THE ULTIMATE GUIDE

to

SELF-DIRECTED RETIREMENT PLANS

Secrets the Rich Use to Build **TAX FREE WEALTH**

THOM GARLOCK

Co-Author of *Trendsetters*

Outskirts Press, Inc.
Denver, Colorado

The investment strategies presented in this book are based upon the research and experiences of the author in his many years as an investor and retirement planning advisor. As you make your own investments, the author and publisher strongly suggest consulting appropriate professionals in the fields of law, taxation, real estate and finance.

Because no investment strategy is foolproof, the authors and publisher are not responsible for any adverse consequences resulting from the use of any of the strategies discussed in the book. When in doubt get competent advice.

COVER DESIGNER: Pamela Trush
TYPESETTER: Delaney-Designs

High Prey Drive Publishing
970 W. Broadway Suite 446
Jackson, WY 83002
800.914.2689

Library of Congress Cataloging-in-Publication Data
Garlock, Thomas W. (Thomas Garlock) 1956-
The Ultimate Guide to Self-Directed Retirement Plans

ISBN: 978-1-4327-9820-8
1. Retirement Accounts 2. Real Estate Investment 3. Tax Savings
Copyright © 2013 by Thomas W. Garlock

The opinions expressed in this manuscript are solely the opinions of the author and do not represent the opinions or thoughts of the publisher. The author has represented and warranted full ownership and/or legal right to publish all the materials in this book.

The Ultimate Guide to Self Directed Retirement Plans
Secrets the Rich Use to Build Tax Free Wealth
All Rights Reserved.
Copyright © 2013 Thom Garlock
V3.0

This book may not be reproduced, transmitted, or stored in whole or in part by any means, including graphic, electronic, or mechanical without the express written consent of the publisher except in the case of brief quotations embodied in critical articles and reviews.

Outskirts Press, Inc.
http://www.outskirtspress.com

ISBN: 978-1-4327-9820-8

Outskirts Press and the "OP" logo are trademarks belonging to Outskirts Press, Inc.

PRINTED IN THE UNITED STATES OF AMERICA

ACKNOWLEDGEMENTS

I want to thank the many people who have shared their IRA and 401(k) investment stories with me. I first want to thank my wife, Karen, for all she has done to make this book a reality and for persevering through the many hours while it was being written.

To write a book like this takes a lot of support and encouragement and I want to thank all the amazing people who surround my life. Of course, to include everyone who has cheered on this effort would take too many pages, but I'd like to thank a few.

Thank you to my parents Richard and Betty for all the encouragement as well as teaching me that there are no limits to what you can do in life when you focus your efforts and refuse to give up. Thank you to Duane Reed for first suggesting I write this book and for all the hours of life and business coaching. Thank you to Katherine Manning for insightful guidance in the creation of this book and for the great job in editing.

Thank you to Al Chariton for introducing me to the world of Self-Directed IRA investing. Much like the people I coach in this area today, I too wish I had started on this path immediately after you first shared with me how powerful it is to manage your own retirement plan.

Thank you to Richard Desich at Equity Trust Co. for all the years of you have dedicated to educating investors on self-directed retirement plans and to Edwin Kelly for the educational events you've organized for the self-directed industry.

A special thanks to Dennis Blitz at The IRA Club for creating as well as hosting so many of the educational events we've presented together over the years and for the guidance on writing this book.

I am very grateful to the wonderful team that works with me every day at IRA Assets and Teton Land Development, including Cyndie Williams, Candy Davis, Iggy Grillo Dylan Leonakadis and Terry

Mortenson. A special thanks to Megan Hill who was instrumental in the early creation and research for this book.

A big thanks to all the real estate investment teachers I've learned from over the years including Dyches Boddiford, Peter Fortunato, John T.Reed and David Tilney. Thank you to Doug Casey and the team at Casey Research for the advice on inflation and owning precious metals.

Thank you to Kevin McMahon for your help in writing this book and guiding me to the publishing team that made it a reality. Thanks to Nick Nanton,Esq. and Greg Rollett at Dicks + Nanton Agency as well as everyone at America's Premier Experts for help in promoting the self-directed retirement plan message.

Lot's of thanks to my mentors, Brian Tracy, Wayne Dyer, Tony Robbins, Robert Kiyosaki, Chet Holmes, Louise Hay and Dennis Waitley who have taught me innumerable lessons and invaluable skills.

-Thom Garlock

INTRODUCTION

If you are like most investors I know, and this includes the thousands of real estate investors I've gotten to know over the years, you may have heard of owning real estate or other alternative assets in your IRA or 401-k plan but don't know anyone who has done it. There is a very good chance that if you *have* asked one of your advisors about moving your retirement plan assets out of the stock market and into real estate you've been told things like, "I've never heard of that" or "It's very complicated" or "You own enough real estate, let's buy more mutual funds." The people we seek investment advice from often have little or no experience in owning alternative assets like real estate in a retirement plan.

The financial industry is structured around commissions and fees that are paid to those who help you manage the funds you've saved for retirement. The vast majority of financial professionals really *want* you to succeed; happy clients refer friends and family members, and the advisors make more money.

However, today's regulations on financial advisors often prohibit them from suggesting anything that has not been approved by the firm they work for and prohibits them from giving advice outside of the specific industry that has issued them a license to do business. These factors means that today's investors must gather their own information, conduct their own research and make decisions often as independent thinkers.

Let's face it, no one cares more about your money and retirement goals than you do, so taking control of one of life's most important events is something no one can entirely do for you.

Congratulations to you for realizing this fact. Many people don't realize that they need to manage their own investment funds to get the best possible results. Since you are holding this book, my guess is that you'd like to be informed of investment options that your advisor or tax professional has not fully explored with you.

ABOUT THIS BOOK

I've consulted with thousands of investors over the years, from beginners with some money in a company 401(k) plan or an IRA considering real estate as a potential investment to some of the wealthiest real estate investors and entrepreneurs in the country. The common thread that all of these investors share, is the desire to improve investment performance leading to a greater net worth so that their retirement years really do become everything they've dreamed of.

"Beginner" investors typically want to find an alternative to stocks, bonds, CDs and mutual funds. "Wealthy" investors have often built their net worth through real estate or a business they started; these folks often want to save taxes by using their retirement plan as an investment vehicle.

This book strives to explain clearly, in layperson's terms, the mechanics and best practices for establishing a Self-Directed IRA that gives you full control over investments you select, manage and profit from, so that when the day comes to truly live off your savings, there will be more than enough to pay for your dreams. You will discover how to diversify, moving away from the standard investment products offered by Wall Street and your local banker, so that your retirement savings not only grows but it grows without the risks that come from letting others manage your money.

This book isn't meant to be read from front to back. (I didn't even write it from front to back.) It's more like a reference. Each chapter is divided into sections, so you can jump in anywhere and find out how to accomplish a specific task or review your options when you come to a fork in your investment road.

My hope is that this book can be used as both a weapon and a shield as you battle against those who will tell you what you've learned here is crazy or impossible or just a bad idea. Since 98% of the population has never heard of investing your retirement plan into real estate or, what Wall Street likes to call other, alternative assets, you may need to protect yourself from those who want to give advice in areas in which they have no experience.

Who should read this book?

This book is for anyone interested in getting the maximum benefits from having a retirement plan, diversifying assets and getting control over the savings intended for retirement.

Some of you include:
- Investors who need to re-build their retirement savings
- Real estate investors - both the beginner and the seasoned professional
- Financial advisors
- CPAs and tax advisors
- Real estate agents and brokers
- Title officers and escrow agents
- Those teaching basic investing classes

Disclaimer

The information in this book is for educational purposes only and should not be construed as investment or tax advice. The author and publishers are not responsible for any losses incurred using any of the strategies described in this book. Please consult with an investment or tax adviser to ensure that any type of investment or retirement plan is suitable for your individual situation.

This work is not intended and should not be relied upon as a professional opinion or advice on any legal, tax or investment aspects of retirement accounts. The list of custodians or service providers in this book is not in any way an endorsement, referral, or analysis as to any firm's financial condition or level of expertise. The author and publisher shall have neither liability nor responsibility to any person or entity with respect to loss or damage caused, or alleged to be caused directly or indirectly by the information contained in this book.

How this book is organized

American consumers have this idea of a perfect retirement lifestyle that has been sold to us by advertisers nearly every day of our lives. Watch any commercial by a leading Wall Street brokerage firm or major insurance company, and you typically see a couple in their sixties walking on the beach, looking very happy and relaxed. All you need to do is let the "experts" manage your money or give you some guidance on the right mix of investments, and you'll reach your retirement goals! I wish it were that easy.

We all want the type of lifestyle we see advertised; however, the task of creating a plan and taking the steps to accomplish the plan is seldom at the top of our "to-do list." With that fact in mind, I have dedicated the first few sections of this book to providing motivation to help get you going and keep you motivated to read those sections that only a tax accountant would typically find exciting.

I understand that there are hundreds of things more exciting than reading the rules on what an IRA can and can't do when it comes to investment options. By design, this book enables you to get as much (or as little) information as you need at any particular moment. Having gotten through college English by reading the jacket blurbs of great novels, I understand the value of strategic skimming.

By design, this book is a reference that you can reach for again and again whenever you encounter a new situation. You will receive a fresh wave of inspiration as you read about others who overcame some of the challenges you may be facing. Gradually, you will build your retirement vehicle to transport you into the successful retirement lifestyle you desire, just like the commercials promise.

CONTENTS

INTRODUCTION

SECTION 1   **Controlling Your Own Retirement Plan**

Chapter 1	Is Your Plan for Retirement in Question?............................	23
Chapter 1.1	Is There a Way Out of this Mess?..	26
Chapter 1.2	The Self-Directed Revolution..	29
Chapter 1.3	Baby Boomers Create Another Wave	31
Chapter 1.4	The End of the "Buy & Hold" Stock Investing Strategy	35
Chapter 1.5	Wall Street Does the "Diversification Shuffle"	38
Chapter 1.6	Controlling Your Own Destiny..	41
Chapter 2	The New Trend in Building Retirement Wealth.................	43
Chapter 2.1	Need Proof this is Legal?	46
Chapter 2.2	What Effect Do Taxes Have on Your Retirement Plan?.........	48
Chapter 2.3	Inflation: Friend or Foe of Our Retirement Plan	50
Chapter 2.4	Will Congress Steal My IRA?	52
Chapter 2.5	Everyday IRA Success Stories	55
Chapter 2.6	The Reasons Against Self-Directing Your Own Retirement Plan	59

SECTION 2   **The ABC's of Retirement Plans**

Chapter 3.0	IRA ABC's..	65
Chapter 3.1	How Do I Get More Money Into My Self-Directed Retirement Plan?	75
Chapter 3.2	What Can I Own in My IRA?..	78
Chapter 3.3	What Assets Can I Not Own In My IRA?	81
Chapter 4	Establishing a Self-Directed IRA or 401(k) Plan	83
Chapter 4.1	Establishing Your Self-Directed IRA	88
Chapter 4.2	How Do I Know the Custodian Won't Rip Me Off?............	91
Chapter 4.3	I Want To Use My Local Bank or CPA As My Custodian...	93

Chapter 4.4	How To Minimize Fees Charged to Your Self-Directed Retirement Account	95
Chapter 5	Transfers From a 401k to an IRA	97
Chapter 5.1	The In-Service Rollover	100
Chapter 6	Checkbook IRA Accounts	105
Chapter 6.1	Checkbook IRAs Make Auction-Buying Easy	109
SECTION 3	**Selecting the Right Investments for Your Retirement Plan**	
Chapter 7	Self-Directed Investment Options	113
Chapter 7.1	Your Investment Options Are Endless	116
Chapter 8	What Types of Real Estate Can I Own in My Retirement Plan?	126
SECTION 4	**Leveraging Your New Knowledge**	
Chapter 9	The Small Differences in IRA Real Estate Investing vs. Traditional Real Estate Investing	135
Chapter 10	How to Own Vacation Rental Properties in the IRA	139
Chapter 10.1	Vacation Rental Success Stories	141
Chapter 11	Withdrawing IRA Owned Real Estate From Your Retirement Plan	145
Chapter 12	Investing Your Retirement Plan in Real Estate	150
Chapter 13	IRA Real Estate Purchase Checklist	152
Chapter 14	Building Your Personal Investment Team	155
Chapter 15	Should I Hire a Property Manager?	158
Chapter 15.1	Property Managers Are a Great Source of Good Deals	160
Chapter 15.2	Interview Questions for Property Managers	162
Chapter 16	IRS Rules for the IRA	164
Chapter 16.1	Use Your Custodian as Your IRA Tax Guide	166
Chapter 16.2	Prohibited Transactions	168
Chapter 16.3	Who Are These Disqualified Parties?	171
Chapter 16.4	I've Broken the Rules-Now What?	174
Chapter 16.5	Valuation of Assets in the IRA	175
Chapter 17	Investing With Other Peoples IRA Accounts	178

Chapter 17.1	Steps to Becoming a Successful Borrower From IRA Investors 180
Chapter 17.2	How to Borrow From IRAs to Fund Your Real Estate or Growing Business.. 183
Chapter 17.3	Building Your Creditability Kit.. 186
Chapter 17.4	Building Creditability With Your Investors...................... 189
Chapter 18	What Come First? Should I Look For the Money or the Deal?... 191
Chapter 19	Owning a Business in Your Retirement Plan................... 194
Chapter 20	Time To Get Started... 198

Additional Resources 201
Index 203

A GLANCE AT WHAT'S INSIDE EACH SECTION

SECTION 1: The Need to Control Your Own Retirement Plan

Before you drive your retirement plan vehicle to success, let's get pointed in the right direction. Forget everything you've heard on how difficult it is to successfully manage your own investment accounts and how it's risky to make your own investment decisions. You'll discover that if you just "Invest in what you already know," the odds of success will tilt in your favor. In other words, all of us have experience in one or more areas that allows us to recognize a "good bargain" from a "bad deal" before we spend our hard-earned cash.

By simply investing in things you already understand and constantly getting "good deals" on the assets you choose to hold in your retirement accounts, your overall investment performance will greatly improve.

We'll cover some recent history of the investment markets and consider ways to stop your savings from slowly leaking out of your accounts and instead grow into a stream of profits that can consistently increase even long after you retire.

SECTION 2: The ABCs of retirement plans

There are many types of retirement plans available so we'll cover the basics on what each plan can and can't do for you. There are IRS rules, and each type of plan has limitations on not only how much you can *contribute* into the account each year but also on what you can *do* with the savings you've accumulated when it's time to withdraw it. The best news is that there is no limit to how much you can accumulate in these accounts. The common thread that runs through all of these retirement plans is that you don't have to pay tax on your profits until you withdraw the money. You'll discover that some accounts never pay tax when you begin to use the funds you've built up through wise investing.

This is the section of the book you'll refer back to as you match new investment opportunities with the different type of accounts you'll control. That's right. If you are like many of my clients, you'll have different types of retirement accounts for different investment goals. You'll see the benefits to holding shorter term, more liquid investments in a Health Savings Account and longer-term investments (depending on your age) in a Traditional IRA or Roth IRA.

You'll see how easy it is to transfer funds away from accounts that offer you very limited choices into retirement accounts you can fully control.

SECTION 3: Selecting the right investments for your retirement plans

Now that you know the mechanics of the various types of retirement plans, you get to go shopping for the right assets to hold inside the accounts. I'll share stories of clients who have had great success managing their own accounts as well as some examples on what not to do with your retirement plans.

Of course there are many new investment books introduced each year, and this book cannot provide the necessary guidance you need in every asset class, so we've put our focus primarily on real tangible assets like real estate, precious metals and assets not typically offered by Wall Street.

SECTION 4: Getting started and leveraging your new knowledge

This section is all about taking the steps to consistently get you into the winner's circle. You'll discover ways to keep your profits growing and your account fees to a minimum. I'll share many of the interesting tricks I've learned from clients and real estate investors (I still learn something from them every time we talk). Checklists, along with a quiz for those of you who want to test your new knowledge, are found in this section. All those important nuggets of information that didn't seem to fit elsewhere in the book but can make a huge difference in your bottom line each year are included in this section.

You'll find an FAQ section in this part of the book. The majority of these questions were taken from the many educational webinars we've hosted over the years.

<u>Note</u>: Things change rapidly in the financial world. The rules around retirement plans can and probably will change over time. Visit: <u>www.IRAassets.com</u> for valuable, free resources updating information in this book. You'll be asked to register on your initial visit and confirm, using your email address. The password is: <u>Self Directed IRA</u>. You can change your password once your registration is complete.

How to contact the author

I welcome feedback from you about this book or the articles you'd like to see from me in the future. You can reach me by writing to: Thom@IRAassets.com. For more information about starting a Self-Directed retirement plan, consulting services, upcoming speaking engagements and other fun and educational stuff, please visit our website at: www.IRAassets.com which contains additional resources and free tools.

Please share your success stories with us. Send your pictures and favorite stories to us or post them on our Facebook site under IRAassets.

SECTION 1

Controlling Your Own Retirement Plan

CHAPTER 1

IS *YOUR* PLAN FOR RETIREMENT IN QUESTION?

It's now reported that over eight thousand Americans retire each day.

Through a combination of procrastination and bad timing, many baby boomers are facing a personal financial disaster just as they're hoping to retire. Ten thousand baby boomers are turning sixty-five every day, a pattern that began in January 2011 and will continue until 2030.

The boomers, who in their youth revolutionized everything from music to race relations, are set to redefine retirement. But a generation that made its mark in the tumultuous 1960s now faces a crisis as it hits its own mid-60s.

"The situation is extremely serious because baby boomers have not saved very effectively for retirement and are still retiring too early," says Olivia Mitchell, Director of the Boettner Center for Pensions and Retirement Research at the University of Pennsylvania.

There are several reasons to be concerned:

- The traditional pension plan is disappearing. In 1980, some 39 percent of private-sector workers had a pension that guaranteed a steady payout during retirement. Today that number stands closer to 15 percent, according to the Employee Benefit Research Institute.

- Reliance on stocks in retirement plans is greater than ever; 42 percent of those workers now have a 401(k) plan. But as we know, the past decade has been a lost decade for stocks, with the Standard & Poor's 500 index posting total returns of less than 4 percent since the beginning of 2000.

- Many retirees banked on their homes as their retirement fund. But the crash in housing prices has slashed almost a third of a typical home's value. Now, 22 percent of homeowners, or nearly 11 million people, owe more on their mortgage than their home is worth. Many are boomers now facing retirement.

- Unlike our parents and grandparents, whose pensions and Social Security promised leisure and comfort in the golden years, baby boomers are realizing they are faced with the responsibility of providing their own leisure and comfort.

Even with the utmost planning, wise savings plans, 401(k)s, Roth accounts, government plans, profit sharing and employee stock plans, most Americans are looking at their retirement savings and asking:

Where'd It All Go? . . Can I Ever Retire? . . Will I Run Out Of Money?

It's a time when trust in Wall Street and our elected leaders is hitting an all-time low. So these are good and reasonable questions to ask. Luckily, there are steps you can take to put your retirement plan back on track.

With the guidance offered throughout this book and our potential to work together one-on-one, you'll not only uncover the answers to these questions but will also discover how easy it can be to build a retirement plan that will benefit you, your family and future generations.

No single solution will fit everyone. However, there are a few basic steps that every investor can take to get back on course to building a retirement plan that will pay you the rewards you've worked so hard to attain.

Yes—

There will be many times along your journey towards retirement (and *afterwards*) when you'll come to that dreaded fork in the road as you face new (potentially confusing) options and are unsure as to which way to turn.

Yes—

It will seem as though everywhere you look, there's a different opinion on the correct path to take—just as there always has been. That's the nature of the investment markets. There will always be someone who is buying while someone else is equally excited and pleased to be selling. Some of the advice will come from those you should be able to trust; however, very often, it will be quite self-serving and delivered from those who simply want to make a sale, even if it sends you off in a more dangerous direction.

How About A New Direction That Gives You More Potential Profits and Far

More Control over Your Money

Millions of American investors already have an IRA or 401(k) plan as a part of their personal financial plan. The tax advantages have made it a wise decision. (No taxes are ever paid on income or gains until a withdrawal of capital from the account upon retirement.) These are "nest egg" accounts have the potential for faster growth and the ability to protect us in our retirement years.

However, millions of investors have been very disappointed in the financial results of their "nest eggs" over the last decade. So much so, that many investors don't even open their monthly account statements when they arrive in the mail. For the majority, realizing how little they actually have saved for retirement is scary. Each statement becomes a monthly reminder that they will run out of savings long before they run out of breath.

Chapter 1.1

IS THERE A WAY OUT OF THIS MESS?

> All life is an experiment. The more experiments you make the better.
> ~Ralph Waldo Emerson

There are many good books out there today that document, in great detail, the events that brought about the collapse of the financial system we began to experience in 2008, so we're not going to share a history lesson here. Looking back on all the events that created the collapse, we now know how fragile the system was and how little those in power did to protect us from what occurred.

Looking back, there were many warning signs and, yes, there were those who sounded the alarm well before the crash. Peter G. Peterson, in his 2004 book *Running on Empty,* wrote:

"America's twin deficits are causing some of the world's shrewdest financial minds to raise alarms. These deficits are so large, and our savings rate so low, that there is a real danger that investors around the world will simply lose faith in the U.S. dollar. America was once the greatest creditor to nations around the globe; it's now the largest debtor nation in the world."

At the time *Running on Empty* was published, our nation's debt was predicted to hit $5 trillion by 2014 if big changes to government spending were not enacted. Today, we have surpassed the $15 trillion level in national debt. Both Democrats and Republicans alike have mortgaged America's future through reckless tax incentives, out-of-control spending and Enron-style accounting tricks by Congress.

These same leaders in Washington enacted programs that stimulated the housing boom by not only allowing unqualified borrowers to obtain a mortgage but by threatening lenders into making loans they wouldn't otherwise approve. Wall Street bankers, always looking for a quick profit, created toxic mortgage pools while regulators stood by and failed to diffuse a ticking time bomb. Insiders in both Washington and Wall Street knew this game would eventually end badly but refused to protect the average investor and the taxpayers.

The 2010 documentary movie *Inside Job,* written & directed by Academy Award- nominated filmmaker Charles Ferguson, clearly shows that Wall Street and Washington were working together to enrich themselves at the expense of the unsuspecting American citizen. Little has changed in the time since these devastating events.

You really are on your own.

Today, more and more investors are seeking to take control of their own financial future. They realize they *really are* on their own, regardless of what the Wall Street advertising and our elected officials tells us.

Throughout this book, we'll be recommending three basic investing concepts that will help you navigate your way to financial success using your retirement plan:

- Diversify: Diversify your investments away from Wall Street and back to Main Street. In other words: "Invest in what you know."

- Inflation: Inflation slowly destroys the purchasing power of your savings. You can leverage the effects of inflation so that you grow your savings instead of losing it.

- Taxes: Use these tax-advantaged accounts to keep more of your gains and accelerate the growth rate of your savings.

In summary, each time you are considering a change in your retirement plan investing strategy, ask yourself these questions:

- Am I investing in something I fully understand or am I simply taking a recommendation from someone who is selling his product?

- Is this new investment helping me diversify assets away from Wall Street?

- How will the future effects of inflation influence this investment?

- Is there a way to delay or eliminate the payment of taxes on this investment?

You may be surprised how many investment options you have that can be answered with an undeniable "YES!" to these questions.

Chapter 1.2

THE SELF-DIRECTED REVOLUTION

> It is well enough that people of the nation do not understand our banking and monetary system, for if they did, I believe there would be a revolution before tomorrow morning.
> ~Henry Ford

Many people hear the term "Self-Directed" IRA and think that it is a special type of IRA.

However, in reality, the IRS does not recognize a "Self-Directed" IRA as a *type* of IRA. Any IRA, whether it be a Traditional IRA, Roth IRA, SEP or SIMPLE IRA can be "Self-Directed." Throughout this book, we'll use the term "Self-Directed" because you, the account owner, are making 100% of the investment decisions.

The financial services industry has never had an incentive to offer a truly Self-Directed retirement plan since they benefit by limiting your investment choices to the products they sell. So, they rarely, if ever, guide you in the direction of buying real estate or other tangible assets in your retirement account. Many financial professionals (primarily because it's not included in their training) aren't even aware of the fact that self-directing your retirement plan is even possible.

The true power of a Self-Directed retirement plan is:

You decide *What* to buy...*When* to Buy...*How much* to Pay...and *When* to Sell.

Self-Directed retirement plans are extremely easy to open and manage. And, you get all the tax benefits of the traditional IRA.

With a Self-Directed Retirement plan, you're no longer at the mercy of a bank or brokerage firm, along with their limitations as to what you can own in your account.

In reality, there are very few things you are prohibited from owning in an IRA, only three asset classes, to be exact:

- Life Insurance
- Stock in an S Corporation
- Collectibles: antiques, rugs, gems, stamps, works of art and numismatic coins. (see Chapter 3.3 for a complete list)

The early adopters of the Self-Directed IRA, nearly 30 years ago, were primarily real estate investors seeking tax-deferred income and capital appreciation by owning:

- Single Family Homes
- Apartment Buildings
- Land
- Commercial Properties
- Mortgages on Real Estate

In Section 3 of the book, you'll discover the many asset classes investors own in their Self-Directed retirement plans.

There is a growing number of financial firms who truly grasp the endless possibilities of the Self-Directed retirement account. Over the years, we've worked with a collection of Custodian firms, led by entrepreneurs who *do* see the extreme value in allowing investors to "Invest in what you know." We continually update the list of Self-Directed retirement plan Administrators and Custodians. If you'd like a copy, simply register (if you are a first-time visitor) at: www.IRAassets.com and type in the phrase <u>Custodian List</u> in the Search Box of the home page.

Chapter 1.3

BABY BOOMERS CREATE ANOTHER WAVE

I'm now going to take you through some of the reasons to diversify your retirement plan assets into what are commonly called "Hard Assets" and show you why real estate really is an essential commodity. These days, with the continued decline in the value of the U.S. Dollar, there are plenty of reasons to be investing in tangible assets, but there's one very good reason that stands out which promotes the idea of the investment in real estate.

What we're up against now is something of a ticking time-bomb. Sad as it may seem, the "forever young-don't-trust-anyone-over-30" generation is about to face a grim reality. With the oldest among them now hitting age 65, the baby-boomer generation is entering what might just about pass for old age.

More specifically, they're becoming eligible for their social security benefits. Some started early retirement between 50 and 55, using their employer-sponsored retirement plan savings. Many more are only now awakening to the need to save for retirement and are frantically following intensive savings programs. Bottom line: the market for 401(k) plans and IRA programs has begun to explode. Most advertising by the financial services industry is focused on this part of the population.

There are two ways to look at this situation. On the one hand, most financial planners are drooling at the prospect of so many lost sheep headed in their direction. Retirement is a scary thought, granted. However, it doesn't help that most people facing retirement these days have lacked the foresight to really prepare for retirement or their savings have been washed away in the last market downturn.

In the United Kingdom a similar scenario has begun. The country currently has a large aged population. Many of these elderly rely on a pension (similar to a social security check) to get by week-to-week, month-to-month. These government payments are supporting the retired population, and the money is coming directly from the taxpayer's pocket. Not enough people have savings to see them through their retirement.

What happens when the government is bound to pay for its aged population? Well, the money comes from the taxpayer, as mentioned. This puts additional pressure on the taxpayers who are already working to make their *own* living and perhaps even supporting a family. The tax payments eat away at their present and future standard of living.

Paying higher taxes during their working life, it's unlikely that the present generation of 20-to-30-year olds is going to have much set aside for their retirement when the time comes. They will have to work more years, and the money they make will have to be stretched even farther. We are entering a vicious cycle as future generations, taxed more and saving less, are going to have to rely more on government assistance than ever before. As the aged population continues to grow (due to people living longer), the strain on the government is only going to increase.

All the while, we must also face the reality of inflation. In the last several decades, the value of money and the value of the US dollar have declined. Ten dollars in the 1990s had the purchasing power of about four bucks in today's economy, and the situation is getting worse. What this means, is that before too long, we're going to realize that what little money we have saved up really isn't going to help us much. As the baby boomers head into retirement, what looked like cozy little nest eggs that would continue growing, are now far from adequate to pay even our health care costs let along allow us to travel and enjoy retirement.

Baby boomers are known for having changed and challenged America at each stage of their lives. They started out by filling hospitals to the max as newborns in the late 1940s. They followed that by crowding schools to overcapacity in the 1950s and 1960s. In the 1970s they created a housing boom. Each time, they made a wave, and the nation, unprepared, was caught off-balance. The wave is now poised to bring great change to the retirement-plan industry in general and to IRA programs in particular. Seventy-six million Americans can call themselves baby boomers — anyone born between 1946 and 1964 – which represents a third of the U.S. population. Forty-six million of them will retire between now and 2014.

Many of these baby boomers have saved a good sum of money for retirement. More specifically, they've saved what *sounds* like a lot of money. The average net worth of families where the head of the household is between the ages of 45 and 55 is over $400,000. In fact, baby boomers will have more money in retirement than did their parents or grandparents—even after inflation adjustments. Yes, it *looks* good.

Unfortunately, though, baby boomers will not do anywhere near as well as their parents when the pre-retirement standard-of-living is compared to the expected standard-of-living after retirement. That's because baby boomers are not as frugal as their parents and may have to cut back a bit more on expenses in retirement than their parents did. Living longer will contribute to baby boomers having a hard time subsisting on their retirement money.

Since 1974, IRAs and the gradual switch from employer-sponsored pension plans to salary deferral plans have significantly influenced the baby boomers' retirement picture. Fifty-four percent of all workers aged forty-five to fifty-five participate in some kind of retirement plan at work. The participation numbers jump when employees are reviewed in categories: 64 percent of full-time wage and salaried workers participate in a retirement plan, and over 70 percent of wage and salaried workers who make more than $50,000 per year participate in these retirement plans.

An American Association of Retired Persons (AARP) study further supports that baby boomers are using retirement plans to save, with 70 percent of baby boomers currently funding IRAs, 401(k) plans or other retirement plans. One estimate of the total assets held in all retirement plans exceeds $12 trillion.

Think about what this money is part of and the bigger picture. The United States currently owes in excess of $15 trillion dollars, and the $12 trillion hoarded away by baby boomers is going to be very much needed for the next 20, 30, or even 40 years as they sidle on through old age.

IRA and 401(k) advertising currently emphasizes growth or tax benefits as the key benefits. Neither the growth nor the benefits are going to be sufficient to help many baby boomers in the long-term when they need it most. Regardless of the numbers reported by our government agencies, inflation is eating away at the purchasing power of the savings these retirees have.

To protect against the devastating effects of inflation, a diversified retirement plan must hold various types of hard assets. The best type of hard assets can often be real estate that pays a monthly or annual income. As the effects of inflation take hold, those who own rental real estate, whether it's residential or commercial property, will be able to raise rents right along with the increases consumers will see on the price of all other goods and services.

Chapter 1.4

THE END OF THE "BUY AND HOLD" STOCK INVESTING STRATEGY

Chains of habit are too light to be felt until they are too heavy to be broken.

~Warren Buffett

Smart investing requires a commitment of your time. You have to monitor the market. It doesn't matter whether its stocks that trade on the US or global markets or real estate in your area. In general, the faster the market moves, the more time it takes to manage. That's why I like real estate. Change in the real estate market often happens slowly, maybe slower than any other market. Some commitment of time must be spent monitoring the market so you know what the current trends are. Knowing the trends helps you get in or out at the best time. When you invest in things you already understand and are monitoring the market because it is of *interest* to you, your performance is bound to be better.

Different Paths to the Same Destination

David is a bright guy who has always worked in Fortune 500 companies as a manager. He has a degree in finance and is a Certified Public Accountant (CPA). He likes trading stocks because he can read the financial statements of companies in which he invests. He spends on average of an hour each day monitoring his stock and options positions. In the years when the stock market is trending upward, he typically does well, making an annual return in excess of 10%, but when the market is trending down like it has over the last decade, he breaks even or sometimes ends the year with a loss. Many years he has nothing to show for his efforts, but he gets a thrill out of the occasional wins he has when he sells a stock at a gain.

And then there's Henry, a bright guy who didn't go to college but instead went to trade school where he learned to become a plumber. After five years working for a local plumbing contractor, he started his own business and now employs eleven workers, including an office manager and a bookkeeper. Henry spends much of his time in homes and commercial buildings, where he oversees plumbing repairs or installations in new construction projects.

His investment preference is real estate. He buys a property only after his research shows he should receive a 12% yield on the invested capital. He factors in vacancy periods and maintenance costs to his estimated costs of ownership. At the end of each year he has something to show for his investment of time. He has made a good return on the invested cash regardless of whether the value of the property has increased or not that year. There are many weeks where Henry doesn't have to spend any time monitoring his rental properties. He has taught his office staff to do most of the work of renting, scheduling repairs and collections, so his time is free to look for more opportunities.

Clearly David and Henry have different investment methods. Neither approach is better than the other, but Henry has never had a year where he hasn't made a return on his invested cash. Slowly but surely, Henry is building wealth. His funds are not directly tied to the daily market gyrations on Wall Street or the global economy. The only trends that Henry needs to monitor are those occurring in his local real estate market.

The "buy and hold" approach to stock investing may have worked many years ago, but in today's global market dominated by hedge funds and computerized trading, it's the stock trader that has the upper hand over the "buy and hold" long-term investor. From Henry's example above, we see that "buy and hold" is working very well in real estate over the long-term as long as there is a good annual yield paid on the invested capital.

Chapter 1.5

WALL STREET DOES THE "DIVERSIFICATION SHUFFLE"

Wide diversification is only required when investors do not understand what they are doing.
~Warren Buffett

Diversification of your investment portfolio into as many different asset classes is your biggest weapon against fighting risk. Unfortunately, however, Wall Street's definition of diversification generally translates into, *"Diversify Only Into What I Sell."* Far too often when an investor seeks advice on diversification into real tangible asset classes, their investment advisor doesn't offer, they hear all the reasons why the diversification strategy doesn't make sense.

Your assets merely being shuffled around, from one mutual fund investment into another isn't true diversification of your savings. True diversification comes from disconnecting a sensible portion of your total savings away from Wall Street based investments.

Building Wealth in Spite of Your Advisor

Meet Ginny, a client from Ft. Lauderdale, Florida she had owned two rentals over the course of her investment career: a single family home she inherited and a high-rise condo overlooking the beach.

Ginny had done well over the years she'd owned these properties, which she leased out on an annual basis. Having earned better and more consistent returns than her stock portfolio ever did, she knew *this* was the road to a more lucrative (and secure) retirement. So, we began our work together by combining three older 401(k) accounts from past employers into a Self-Directed IRA account with a local custodian she selected. Ginny's goal was to purchase a single family home in an affordable neighborhood and hold it as a rental property, after completing some cosmetic improvements to the property.

After shopping for the perfect property, she received news from her Realtor that her purchase offer on a three-bedroom, two-bath home was accepted and would be ready to rent after the renovation was completed.

Feeling very excited about her upcoming investment, Ginny headed downtown to share the good news with her advisor. Being that he had been a family friend, long before he ever became her stockbroker, he was one of the first people with whom she wanted to share the news of her new investment.

Right off, the drama began:

- He dug up extremely old statistics on which he based dire predictions of horrific losses to come in the real estate sector.

- He questioned if the use of a Self-Directed IRA was even legal.

- He felt the risks of being a landlord were too great for a single woman.

- His advice was to cancel the deal and, instead, buy a real estate mutual fund.

Ginny was disappointed as well as angry and rightfully so. The account her stockbroker had managed was up only 11% over the last ten years. With an average annual yield of just over 1% she wasn't going to be able to someday live off of the savings in her account, at least not for very long!

Stockbrokers are rarely educated on the advantages of a Self-Directed retirement plan, unless it's a product offered by their firm. Many of the larger discount brokerage firms have begun labeling their various retirement plan offerings as "Self-Directed" accounts, and they *are* as long as you select only from their list of approved stocks, bonds or mutual funds.

Ginny discovered the Self-Directed IRA through her own research. She decided to take control of her future retirement plans and invest in assets she fully understood. She gathered her own real estate market data, hired a good Realtor and ended up with a property that will generate good annual yields many times greater than her portfolio of stocks and mutual funds.

Financial returns are often much higher when investors discover they can place their retirement funds into assets they understand and over which they have more control.

Chapter 1.6

CONTROLLING YOUR OWN DESTINY

Formal education will make you a living; self-education will make you a fortune.

~Jim Rohn

It's very safe to say that no one cares more about your money than you do. None of us would hand over our wallet to a stranger and ask him to return it in a week, but it's so common to hand our retirement funds to an advisor, who in turn invests it into a mutual fund which is managed by someone we can't name, who then invests the funds into a company we've never heard of, that operates in an industry we can't begin to understand.

It's a sad but true fact that too often the mutual funds that end up in our retirement plans are recommended because they pay the highest fees to the person selling us the funds. The mutual fund managers buy stocks that appear to have the best short-term odds of performing since managers are graded upon not just their annual performance but, more importantly, their quarterly performance.

The entire system needs an overhaul. Unfortunately, that's not going to happen since too many in the financial services industry are earning their paychecks from the system that's in place today. They get paid whether you win or lose. Efforts to reform the system are made merely by politicians making noise in an effort to garner votes or attract campaign contributions from lobbyists.

The financial services industry has been very effective at convincing generations that investing is complicated and you can't possibly do this on your own. Is there any wonder they don't teach basic household financial management in high school? They want to keep the majority of investors reliant upon hiring an outsider to manage their finances.

For many years now, the majority of mutual fund managers haven't been able to beat the performance of the market indexes with any regularity, yet most investors turn their hard-earned savings over to an investment manager.

Growth in Self-Managed Portfolios

The self-managing trend is not new. From the beginning days of trading on Wall Street, there have always been those who managed their own stock portfolio. With the advent of the discount brokerage firm in the mid-70s, more and more investors, determined to grow their wealth, have discovered they could manage their own investment portfolio and still have time for a normal life.

Today, investors have discovered that to truly diversify and grow their wealth, they need to move some portion of their retirement funds away from the global equities market that has become heavily dominated by hedge funds and computerized trading, into real tangible assets they can control. It's hard to imagine that the average investor today has any consistent advantage over Wall Street money managers, but when it comes to local markets, the smaller independent investor gains a large and often consistent advantage over Wall Street.

When it comes to managing the most important portion of your investment portfolio, your retirement funds, my best advice is to own assets that you, without question, understand and control. The Self-Directed IRA or 401(k) is the vehicle of choice for those who are willing to accept the responsibility of building wealth that will be there when they need it most.

Nothing is more rewarding in the investment game than tasting success that's been achieved from your own research and management of the assets you've selected.

Chapter 2

THE NEW TREND IN BUILDING RETIREMENT WEALTH

Wealth is not his that has it, but his that enjoys it.
~Benjamin Franklin

I could fill an entire book with success stories of those who have taken control of their retirement funds, doing what their advisors warned them *not* to do. Some of the most important stories, however, are those that reveal what happened to those who didn't follow a well-thought-out plan. I'll be sure to share the stories of failure (so we can learn from the mistakes of others) as well as the stories of success throughout this book. Here are two success stories to get us started on what can happen when you combine a good plan with the right actions.

Bill and Donna are in their early 30's and the proud parents of two young, very energetic boys. They met while working at a Dotcom company. This company was very generous issuing company stock into their 401k plans prior to the company's IPO in the late 90's. Like many young workers in their industry, before the tech bubble burst, they couldn't believe how quickly their net worth had grown. When their company had to merge with a competitor after the market crash, both Bill and Donna still had good middle-management jobs but their account values had dropped by 70%. Fortunately for them, their new employer offered them the option to either rollover their old 401k into the new employer plan or transfer their 401k account to an IRA.

This is when they discovered the Self-Directed IRA that would allow them to purchase real estate. In an effort to diversify their investments into assets they could better control, they began with buying a single-family home. It was in need of cosmetic repairs but close to their home in Dallas, Texas.

Like most first-time remodel investors, they'll tell you they spent too much on making the home perfect again, but when they sold it for a $23,000 net profit they knew this was something they'd want to do again and again.

By using their Self-Directed IRA funds, they avoided paying any taxes on every dollar of profit earned on each of their property sales. Their retirement savings have grown much faster by owning their real estate investments in a tax-advantaged account vs. investing non-retirement plan capital. Bill and Donna had to make sure they didn't break any of the IRS rules that govern holding real estate in an IRA (I'll cover the common rookie mistakes in a minute) and have had a lot of fun turning ugly homes into beautiful homes that sell quickly and generate annual returns between 12% to 20% into their IRA accounts.

In the last two years, Bill and Donna have added a new approach to their real estate investment business. Since they feel inflation is the next long-term economic trend that threatens our economy, they have chosen to buy and then rent the homes they purchase with their Self-Directed accounts. Their rental income now flows tax-free back into their IRA accounts each month. Over time the property values, along with the monthly rents, will most likely increase and keep pace with inflation.

Eventually, their IRAs will own several rental properties free of any debt and generate a strong steady cash flow during retirement.

Much of their success is tied back to using their IRA funds in areas not directly connected to the traditional Wall Street investing approach.

The "I don't want Tenants" approach

Some investors just don't want the responsibility of being a landlord. They are either too busy or believe that spending time managing their own properties is just not a productive task.

That brings us to the story of Ed, a retired quality control manager who spent most of his career working in the aircraft manufacturing industry. Years ago, he tried managing a rental property he had once lived in after his family outgrew the house that he and his wife Liz bought after they were married. Ed just couldn't get along with his tenants, he tells me, because they didn't take the best of care of his property.

Before he retired, Ed came to me when researching the Self-Directed IRA, because he had built up an average sized 401k plan over his career. He was very clear he didn't want to spend his retirement years managing tenants; however, he was also very clear that he wanted to diversify his nest egg into real estate.

I'll never forget Ed's primary reason for wanting real estate investments in his retirement plan. He felt that the recession we were in at the time could only be resolved by returning the U.S. to that of a strong exporter nation, again. To accomplish that goal, he felt the value of the U.S. Dollar would be destroyed by those in Washington in an effort to stimulate the economy and greater job growth. That's a pretty safe bet when you realize the U.S. Dollar has lost value nearly every year for the last 98 years. Ed saw the value of owning real tangible assets that he could control, in his retirement plan. I couldn't agree more with his analysis and plan of action. For several years now he has relied upon property managers to oversee his portfolio of properties with good success.

As I mentioned earlier, I'll share stories that are sure to get you thinking of ways you can use a self-directed retirement plan to build your wealth with more control and far less risk than the traditional approach to investing retirement funds.

Chapter 2.1

NEED PROOF THIS IS LEGAL?

When people initially hear about the concept of the self-directed IRA, they are often naturally skeptical, believing it too good to be true. Being able to invest in what you know and are familiar with vs. owning Wall Street-sponsored investments does sound pretty good!

The good news is that this is not too good to be true. In fact, since the IRA was created in 1974, investing in real estate and other alternative assets has been legal. Each year, the IRS Publication 590 (Visit: www.IRS.gov) updates many of the important guidelines, including annual contribution limits and how to take withdrawals, as well as a detailed description of which investments are prohibited. As we mention in Chapter 3.3, these investments include artwork, stamps, rugs, antiques, gems and antique cars. All other investments, including stocks, bonds, mutual funds, real estate, mortgages, private stock and other hard assets like precious metals are acceptable, as long as the IRS rules governing retirement plans are followed.

The reason most investors and financial professionals are not aware of this opportunity is because most IRA custodians or financial service firms do not offer truly self-directed IRA accounts that allow you to invest in real estate and other non-traditional investments.

Most custodians, when asked, "Can I invest in real estate with an IRA?" will answer, "Sorry, we've never heard of that" or "No, we don't allow that type of investment." In reality, their response should be, "We allow only the products we offer, like stocks, mutual funds, bonds or CDs to be owned by the IRA."

It's because of this common miscommunication that so many investors and their advisors have held the opinion that the IRA is simply an investment vehicle for paper assets like stocks, bonds and mutual funds.

The rapidly growing trend to self-direct one's retirement plan has not gone unnoticed by the Wall Street marketing machine. Many of the large discount brokerage firms have, in the last few years, begun calling their IRA and 401(k) plans "self-directed" which in their perspective means clients are allowed to move funds between the collection of stocks, bonds, mutual funds and money market funds the firms offer.

Occasionally, I'll receive a call from an investor who wants to own real estate in his IRA and is looking for clarification because an IRA custodian at a discount brokerage firm has said that his self-directed IRA cannot buy real estate with funds in a retirement plan.

At the end of the day, the custodian for your retirement plan can and does dictate what they are willing to allow you to hold as an investment in your retirement plan. The solution for many investors today is to seek out a custodian who will allow a much broader choice of investment opportunities; this will give you true diversification of your retirement funds.

Chapter 2.2

WHAT EFFECT DO TAXES HAVE ON YOUR RETIREMENT PLAN?

"Compound interest is the most powerful force on Earth."
~Albert Einstein

One of the most successful real estate investors I know will often ask an audience, "What would you rather have?: A million dollars today or a penny that doubles in value every day for 30 days?" It's one of those trick questions everyone can answer correctly when you think about the answer. Of course the correct answer is the penny that doubles each day for a month, since that calculation totals $5,368,709.

Now, think about what you would have left if you paid the standard income tax on your gain every time the penny doubled. Not a fun math exercise! But this is exactly what happens to your investment gains every time you make a profit. Using this example, if the IRS were to take its typical cut out of your daily gains, you would be left with only $563.47!

This is one of the best justifications I've seen for using an IRA or 401k plan as your preferred investment vehicle. If that penny were doubling each day in such a retirement vehicle, you'd still have every penny of that $5.3 million in your account. Here's why:

Compound interest occurs when you not only earn interest on your original investment sum, but also on the interest earned on the original sum.

For example, beginning at age 25, if you take the $4 you spend each day for coffee and put it towards your retirement savings, you'd save $120 a month, or $1,440 each year. Doesn't sound like a lot at first, but it begins to grow with compounding interest.

If you received 9% in compounding interest each year, you would have $23,317 after 10 years. After 20 years, you'd have $77,076 and after 30 years, at age 55, you'd have an amazing $204,346.

The power of compound interest is multiplied in tax-advantaged accounts.

For example, if you were to contribute $5,000 each year into a tax-advantaged account (an IRA or 401(k)) and assume an 8% compound interest rate of return for 30 years, your Self-Directed IRA would be worth $570,142 at the end of year 30.

If you made the same investment in a non-tax sheltered account, assuming a 25% tax rate, it would be worth $233,343 instead of $570,142. The *effort* on your part is the same under both scenarios. You are saving $5,000 per year and earning a return of 8%. By simply making your investments through a tax-advantaged account, you end up with more than $336,000 of additional savings for a better retirement lifestyle.

In summary, if your plan is to have a million-dollar nest egg to draw upon in your retirement years, reaching that goal is far easier if you do so in a tax-advantaged account. The Self-Directed IRA can be your most important wealth building account. As you'll see in the next chapter, you'll need to protect your nest egg from the dangerous effects on inflation.

Chapter 2.3

INFLATION: FRIEND OR FOE OF YOUR RETIREMENT PLAN

> By a continuing process of inflation, government can confiscate, secretly and unobserved, an important part of the wealth of their citizens.
> ~John Maynard Keynes

For as long as I can remember, the term "inflation" has meant the increase in the prices we pay for goods and services. During the first oil embargo in 1974, we sat in line waiting for our turn to fill our gas tanks while the news on the radio reported how the hike in gas prices would cause inflation. Since then, we have linked price increase with inflation and price declines with deflation. Inflation is actually the increase in money supply, or in other words, an increase in how many U.S Dollars are circulating in the marketplace. So when the financial news reports, "The Federal Reserve will be keeping interest rates low for the foreseeable future because they see no signs of inflation," don't believe it! *It's the Federal Reserve that is creating and managing the money supply, so how can they* not *see signs of inflation?*

Any basic economics book will give you the true definition of inflation. If you compare an older version of Webster's dictionary to a current copy, you'll see that in the 1920s inflation was defined as the "increased issue of paper currency" as opposed to the current definition of "a continuing increase in general price levels." Regardless of which definition you want to use, there has been a tremendous increase in the amount of U.S. Dollars in the system and that's why we have seen the value of the U.S. Dollar decline over the last 10 years. That's why anything you purchase today is far more expensive than it was 10-20 yrs ago.

Investors who have realized the true definition of inflation have done very well to own gold over the last five years. Technically, gold has not increased in price during this time, it just takes far more dollars to buy an ounce. Gold reflects the decline in purchasing power of the dollar. Many experienced investors are now buying real estate as a way to store their wealth until the average investor awakens to the reality that the dollars they hold in CDs and Treasury bills have been losing value each time the Federal Reserve floods the system with more and more dollars to stimulate the economy out of the current slump. I believe we will see an ever-increasing loss in purchasing power of our dollar this decade; owning real assets such as real estate or precious metals in your IRA is the best way to protect what you have.

Planning to Maximize Savings

As April 15th approaches each year, it is time to do what you still can to reduce your tax bill. Among the best ways to boost your nest egg while trimming your taxes is to make the biggest tax-deductible retirement-plan contributions you can. (Check out the IRS website to find updated contribution limits each year.)

Even if you are covered by an employer plan, you may still be able to put money into a Traditional or Roth IRA, up until you file your current year's tax return. (See the contribution tables in chapter 3)

Most financial experts agree that tax rates in the not-too-distant future will rise, while the deductions most high-earners have counted on in the past are being slowly eliminated. With a little study of the retirement plan options available, you will find the plan that fits your needs and be on your way to building an account you can manage with ease.

Chapter 2.4

WILL CONGRESS STEAL MY IRA?

> Washington, DC is to lying what Wisconsin is to cheese.
> ~Dennis Miller

With all of the government bailouts over the past few years, many investors who have diligently worked to build their retirement plans have posed the question of government confiscation of IRAs, as well as other retirement plans, in an attempt to pay the federal debt. This question was rarely asked until the debt levels began to skyrocket after the bailouts beginning in 2008.

With over $5 trillion currently invested in IRA accounts and possibly twice that amount in 401k plans, any politician seeking votes from those in favor of the redistribution of wealth, has been listening to ideas on how to get this capital under their control. Anything is possible, so I won't rule out an attempted takeover of these retirement assets. However, I don't believe we will see an abrupt end to IRA or 401(k) retirement plans but instead, I expect congress will create some very well-crafted incentives for the public to invest their retirement savings into a new breed of retirement account. Don't be surprised that these new accounts will be somewhat limited to primarily owning government issued securities, that will help shift our nations debt into the hands of it's citizens as opposed to other nations around the world.

The type of incentives being considered are rumored to be tax-free distributions from the retirement plan on capital invested into Treasury bills and bonds issued by the federal or state agencies. These types of assets have never been the most popular investments to hold in a tax-advantaged account because they were designed more for income than for long-term growth. In addition, interest earned on these types of investments have typically been tax free, therefore it made little economic sense to hold them in a retirement plan. That won't stop our elected officials in Washington from trying to sell the public on stuffing their retirement plans with "safe" investments thus creating a way for Congress to finance their continued spending.

Protection from confiscation

I don't want to sound alarmist, however, so many clients have been concerned with finding ways to protect the savings they've accumulated in their retirement plans that this would be a good time to share some ideas on how you can insulate yourself from a potential government raid on retirement plans. Of course the unexpected can and does happen especially when we as a country face limited options on how to finance our current national debt levels.

The solution for many investors is to manage their own self-directed retirement plan that holds real estate, precious metals and other non-publicly traded assets. It appears the federal government would have a much harder time getting their hands on the title to real property than they would the mutual funds or bank deposits held in an IRA.

If the real estate held in the retirement plan has a lien on it from a lender, the lender has a security interest in the property making it even harder to lose in a confiscation. When we saw the federal government outlaw the ownership of gold in 1933, citizens were required to simply take their gold to their local bank for an easy exchange into U.S. Dollars.

Regardless of what party may control Washington politics at any given time, I think you'll agree that confiscation of retirement plans would be a ridiculous way to get votes, regardless of the crisis that may be used to justify such action. However, many investors believe this could definitely happen, and they are buying assets outside of the U.S. that can be legally held in their retirement plan. Many of these investors will tell you their primary motive, in owning property offshore, is that it's done for the potential high returns that can be found in emerging markets. I believe their true motive is to move their retirement plan assets further out of reach from the U.S. government.

Whether it's beachfront property in Belize or agricultural land in Brazil, the attraction is that U.S. government would have a difficult time seizing the asset in a confiscation effort to pay off our national debt.

I'm from Washington and here to help you!

Don't be surprised to see more calls for a government-managed retirement system during the next financial crisis. Many in Washington believe they know what is best for the average citizen, and they'd like to take the burden of investment management off your back and help you save for the future. There certainly is a segment of our population that will find the offer attractive.

The Roth conversion rules that were so popular in 2010 generated a windfall of tax revenue to the Treasury. As investors paid their taxes early upon converting their traditional IRAs and 401k plans into Roth accounts, these investors were in effect making an early tax payment that was not due until they reached retirement age and began making their withdrawals.

For Uncle Sam, this was like finding a $20 bill in a pair of favorite jeans after they'd been through the laundry. Expect more creative incentives out of Washington when it comes to the rules on converting to the Roth IRA, as well as whatever new breed of retirement plan is created by Congress. We've seen just the tip of the Roth conversion incentive iceberg in my opinion.

In summary, I believe it is unlikely that we will see a direct government attempt to convert our retirement plans into a new slush fund. We will, however, see more and more tinkering with the incentives to pull our savings from our retirement plans and pay the taxes now versus in the future.

Chapter 2.5

EVERYDAY IRA SUCCESS STORIES

Develop success from failures.
Discouragement and failure are two of the surest stepping stones to success.
~Dale Carnegie

Before we get into all the ways to take control of your retirement plan and the methods used by successful self-directed investors, I'd like you to read about a few I've had the pleasure of meeting. One could easily fill a book with success stories alone; I am going to share with you, the methods they have used to build wealth with their retirement plan. In the chapters ahead, we will cover both the successful systems as well as the investing mistakes that are common when using an IRA or 401k plan. The goal at this point is to show you that investors *without* a great deal of capital or special skills are building retirement plans they can count on in the future, without the risks that are so prevalent when one puts all their funds into the hands of Wall Street.

My editor had a great idea that will help you, the reader, gain as much as possible, in the least amount of time, from the many client stories in this book. Everyone is at a different point in their investing journey. Though it may be fun to share in the success of a new investor, we realize many of you are extremely experienced and are seeking ways to continue your successful investing methods, by using an IRA or 401(k) plan to minimize or eliminate taxes on your profits.

Other readers are early in their journey and need to build a strong foundation of skills so they can avoid possible pitfalls along the way. Then, there are those of you who have experience but feel you have even more to learn.

Because we don't know which category you fit into, we segmented the stories into three types of investors: The Rookie, The Semi-Pro and the Pro. Pick the category you feel best represents you and review these stories, feeling free to skip those that may not provide as much value to you.

For example, if after reading the descriptions below, you identify most with "The Pro" because you've been a real estate investor for many years, the stories about "The Rookie" investors may not have tremendous value, other than bringing back memories of your early real estate transactions. However, if you've yet to gain much experience as a real estate investor, I think you'll find each of the investor stories have something to offer. In the end, my goal is to move you to the next level and improve your overall investment results.

The Rookie

Sam and Amy are a young couple in their late 20's with 2 young children. They love to find older homes that are in disrepair and make them beautiful again. Although a real estate agent helped them purchase the first few homes they remodeled, they have recently begun buying homes owned by local banks that had acquired them through the foreclosure process. They quickly learned what many seasoned real estate investors will tell you is the secret to real estate investing: "You make your money when you buy, and you receive the profit when you sell" which simply means you have to get a good deal on the property at the time of purchase. Sam and Amy didn't start with a large sum of capital when they began buying homes. Sam had $15,000 in an IRA, and Amy had less than $5,000 in a 401k plan from a prior employer.

Sam and Amy saw the value of sharing their opportunities with others and used that knowledge to finance their part-time business. They contacted people they knew with IRA accounts that were not earning much in money market funds or certificates of deposit. Then, they formed small partnerships, combining their funds to buy homes which they repaired and then sold for a nice profit. After a few years, they had done just about every type of partnership arrangement you can imagine. Sometimes the profits on the sale of a property were split 50/50 while other times, their partner was paid a fixed amount of profit for providing the necessary capital.

The Semi-Pro

Jerry is a 40-year-old electronics engineer in Dallas, Texas, who has been buying and managing rental properties for the last 6 years. Since managing his real estate portfolio is not his full-time job, he falls into the Semi-Pro category. Jerry's goal is to generate strong monthly cash flow from his rentals with the least amount of time spent on management duties. His first four properties were purchased outside of his retirement plan. After he exhausted those *personal* cash reserves, he began researching ways to invest the savings in his company-provided 401(k) plan. Fortunately, his employer's plan allowed him to complete an "in-service rollover" of funds from his 401(k) into a Self-Directed IRA. (see Chapter 5.1 on In-Service Rollovers)

Because Jerry manages his own rental properties, he elected to open what is commonly called a "Checkbook IRA" so he could administer all the banking activities himself. This approach saves potential delays when working with his custodian to deposit monthly checks from his tenants and allows Jerry to pay all the property expenses, since he writes all the checks himself from the IRA account. (see Chapter 6 on Checkbook IRAs)

Jerry has focused his energy over the last few years on buying properties at the County foreclosure auction in order to get the best possible price. He is quick to admit his risks are higher since he seldom has the opportunity to fully inspect the property in advance of the auction sale however, he knows his market well and he can spot a bargain property regardless of the repairs that may be needed before it is rentable.

He does all of his own tenant screening and property maintentence in an effort to generate the highest possible return on his investments.

The Pro

Roger is one of the many Pros I've had the pleasure of working with and learning from. He sold his manufacturing company several years before we met and began buying real estate close to his home in Boise, Idaho. What started as a part-time investment into single-family homes has grown into owning garden apartment complexes in several states.

Roger has mastered the art of team building and attributes most of his success to the members of his team.

I really didn't realize it at the time, but when he first contacted me he was in need of someone to add to the team he had built. The problem that Roger faced, like so many successful investors, was that he was paying a great deal of taxes on the profits he earned from owning rental real estate. To minimize those taxes, Roger completed an "exchange" each time he sold a property vs. paying the taxes at the time of each sale. (see Chapter 9 on 1031 exchanges).

Like any good team leader or captain, Roger looked as far as he could into the horizon to see what may be in his future. He didn't like what he saw.

He realized that by constantly orchestrating an "exchange" each time he sold a property, he was only delaying the payment of tax. Someday, those taxes would need to be paid if he ever expected to sell his properties and live off of the savings he had accumulated. Roger began researching ways to use his 401(k) plan as a vehicle to own real estate, since he could receive rental income and the gains from each property sale without immediately paying taxes.

Roger realized each member of his team had a role, and the team is only as good as its weakest player. Roger's goal was to continuously improve his team, as he knew that would lead to better performance, which in this game translates to better net returns.

The team members now include: a CPA, an IRA custodian and several real estate brokers, property managers, lenders and me, his real estate retirement plan advisor. It's amazing to see how easily Roger is able to manage his numerous properties without spending all his time buried under the weight of the day-to-day operations of his real estate business. Instead, he keeps his focus on managing the *team* rather than each of his properties.

In chapter 14, I'll share with you everything I've watched Roger and many other Pros do, on a consistent basis, to build wealth through building a good team.

Chapter 2.6

THE REASONS AGAINST SELF-DIRECTING YOUR OWN RETIREMENT PLAN

Things done well and with a care, exempt themselves from fear.
~William Shakespeare

Like so many other decisions you'll make as an investor, there are both positive and negative factors to explore when taking the self-directed retirement plan approach. I want to make sure you come away with a clear understanding of the possible negatives to using a Self-Directed IRA or 401(k) plan. This approach is certainly not for everyone.

For many generations now, the Wall Street marketing machine has convinced us that in order to call yourself an "investor," you have to own a collection of stocks, bonds or mutual funds, offered by a firm that has done much of the research and can help you make the best choices in a very complicated marketplace. For example, nearly mutual funds come with a 1-to-5-star rating based on how well the manager has performed in up-and-down markets, as well as how their fees compare to other management firms.

It wasn't until the mid-70s that discount brokerage firms were established and began promoting the idea that average investors could do their own research and make their own decisions on what stocks or mutual funds to buy. Now that we are in a global market with far more investment options than ever before, the idea of giving your money to a professional to manage is perceived to be the wise and prudent approach.

If you lack the confidence to make your own informed investment decisions, even after you've completed your own research, which may include advice from Wall Street's best and brightest managers, then taking on the responsibility of managing your own investments may be too big of a step for you.

In my experience, there are many investors who, even after conducting their own research, just aren't comfortable making their own investment decisions. Maybe they need someone to blame if things don't work out or they struggle with the fact that their actions could lead to a loss of precious capital they will need to rely upon during retirement their retirement years. The possibility of making a mistake drives them to hire an investment manager or financial planner who can hopefully help them grow their funds for a better life tomorrow.

Self-directing your own retirement plan should not be attempted by those who have difficulties taking responsibility for their own choices. Much has been written about the need for social confirmation of our decisions when it comes to our investment choices. Unfortunately, the majority of investors who wait for all of their friends to invest in an asset class before they join in are the ones who repeatedly buy in at the top of a market before the bubble bursts. They seldom make consistent profits. The investor who often takes a contrarian approach to the market, regardless of what asset class they select, is the one who most often outperforms those who run with the herd. If you are reluctant to invest in an asset class when you don't see those around you doing so, then self-directing your retirement plan may not be an option you should consider.

The other type of investor I would discourage from the self-directed approach is the one who just won't commit the time and energy to managing his own finances. With a Self directed IRA or 401(k) plan, there comes a level of responsibility to keep your funds working and growing. I've never heard of a self-directed custodian contacting an account holders to remind them that cash is sitting idle in their account and should be invested somewhere for a higher return. I understand there are also those who earn substantial amounts of income in their selected profession, and they just lack the time to manage their own investments. You may truly desire higher returns from your retirement plan than those your advisor has delivered, however, if you can't commit the time to managing the funds, you are better off looking for a new advisor as opposed to taking on the task of self-managing your own account.

Fortunately, you don't have to make the switch to self-directing 100% of your retirement funds. Initially, it is often best to "test drive" the self-directed approach with a single investment or two. Start small with investments you understand, to test the waters. You can always go back to what you've been doing if the self-directed approach is not a good fit for you. Again, I always recommend keeping the existing IRA account you already have established with a brokerage firm (just keep a small balance in the account) vs. closing out the account and transferring all of your funds to a new self-directed custodian. This gives you the option to transfer your funds back if for any reason the self-directed method isn't a good fit for you.

SECTION 2

The ABCs of Retirement Plans

Chapter 3.0

IRA ABC'S

Recognizing that we all have different situations and are in different stages in our retirement planning process and seeing as there are several retirement plan account options, let's start with some basic and very important information.

What is an IRA?

IRA stands for Individual Retirement Arrangement. Put simply, it's a savings account for retirement that offers some tax advantages. These tax advantages occur either at the time contributions are made into the account or at the time funds are withdrawn from the account during retirement.

Regardless of when you receive a tax deduction or get access to tax-free income, these benefits are secondary to the fact that all earnings derived from assets held in the account are tax-free in the year they occur. In other words, there is (1) no limit to the amount of profit you can earn from the investments that are held in the account and (2) no requirement to pay tax on the earnings in the year(s) the gains occur.

There are many investors who have an IRA but have seldom seen it as their most valuable vehicle to building retirement wealth. Because all of us are limited in what we can deposit into our IRA each year and, more importantly, because these accounts haven't built a reputation for rapid wealth accumulation, they are often neglected savings accounts.

Many investors tell me that their 401(k) plans have been given more attention over the years simply because those accounts boast a larger balance. Many of these people have recently changed jobs and now have the freedom to transfer their 401(k) funds into an IRA; they see the self-directed IRA option as a good way to diversify their savings into investment choices of their own.

What are the different types of IRAs?

There are four different types of IRA accounts:

Roth IRA
- contributions are made with after-tax capital
- all earnings within the Roth IRA have no tax impact
- Withdrawals from the account are tax-free

Traditional IRA
- contributions are made with pre-tax capital
- contributions are typically tax-deductible
- all earnings within the traditional IRA have no tax impact
- withdrawals from the account are taxed as income

SEP IRA
- allows a small business or self-employed person to make a tax-deductible contribution into a retirement plan
- all contributions are made by the employer
- both employer and employee contributions can be made each year but are not mandatory

Simple IRA
- allows both employer and employee contributions, similar to a 401(k) plan but with lower contribution limits
- both employer and employee contributions can be made each year but are not mandatory; business owners with 100 or fewer employees are eligible

All of the above retirement plans can be self-directed depending on the custodian you select when the plan is established. Most custodians for self-directed retirement plans offer all of the above types of plans.

There is no good or bad choice to make here. The type of IRA that you select must match your needs and investment objectives. There is no restriction on the number of IRA accounts any individual can have, however, there are annual contribution limits. Your CPA or tax advisor can help you determine your maximum contribution limit each year. Annual contribution limits have been increasing over time, and those over 50 years of age are given the ability to contribute more into their accounts.

The chart below describes the important features of each type of IRA account:

Account Type	Maximum Annual Contribution Limit	Additional Contributions for People Age 50 Years & Older
Traditional IRA	$5,000	$6,000
ROTH IRA	$5,000	$6,000
SEP IRA	20% of net self-employment income (or 25% of compensation) up to $49,000	None
Simple IRA	$11,500	$2,500
Solo 401K*	20% of net self-employment income (or 25% of compensation) plus $16,500 up to $49,000	$5,500
ROTH 401K*	20% of net self-employment income (or 25% of compensation) plus $16,500 up to $49,000	$5,500

Roth IRA Accounts

The Roth IRA is a retirement plan that accepts post-tax income. Therefore, contributions are not tax-deductible. However, since the account owner has already paid income tax on each contribution before the deposits are made, no tax is due as the funds are withdrawn during retirement. This makes the Roth IRA unique when compared to other retirement plans and for most investors, the most powerful retirement planning vehicle available.

Like other IRAs, the Roth can be own a wide variety of assets, including stocks, bonds, mutual funds, CDs and tangible assets like real estate and precious metals.

As always, there are contribution limits imposed by the IRS Code. In the case of the Roth IRA, annual contributions are capped to the lesser of your taxable compensation. This means if you do not have earned income because you are retired or you are a small businesses owner who has not received a paycheck during the year, you are not eligible to make contributions to a Roth IRA account.

Distributions from earnings are federally tax-free if you've had your Roth IRA for at least five years and you're over age 59½ or, if you are under age 59½, have had your Roth IRA for at least five years, and the distribution is due to your death or disability. Distributions also are tax-free for a first-time home purchase ($10,000 lifetime maximum).

In essence, the Roth IRA provides investors with a hedge against future tax increases, thereby providing an effective tool for managing their income during retirement.

Roth IRA Advantages

First-Time Homebuyer Benefit

The Roth IRA owner may withdraw up to $10,000 in earnings tax-free if the money is used to purchase a principal residence for the account owner, a spouse, descendants or lineal ancestors, providing the recipient has not owned a residence in the previous two years.

Multiple Retirement Account Benefit

Owning a Roth IRA does not prevent an owner from also participating in a 401(k) plan.

Distribution Benefit

The Roth IRA is the only plan that does not require distributions to begin on an IRS determined age threshold. For example, a traditional IRA requires withdrawals to begin when the owner reaches age 70 ½. These distributions are known as required minimum distributions (RMDs), and IRS penalties are levied on those who fail to make a required withdrawal. Many successful investors I've worked with don't need the income from their traditional IRAs when they reach age 70 ½, but have no choice but to make the RMD and pay the taxes due. A Roth IRA has advantages if you wish to pass along a portion of your wealth to your family.

Death Benefit

In the event that a Roth IRA owner dies and the beneficiary already owns a separate Roth IRA, the beneficiary is permitted to combine the accounts without penalty. However, beneficiaries who inherit a Roth IRA are subject to minimum distribution rules.

Contribution Limit Benefit

This benefit is very simple. Both Roth and traditional IRAs have the same annual contribution limits. Since the amount invested in a Roth is post-tax, the effective net value of the funds in a Roth IRA is greater than that in a traditional IRA, thereby making the Roth IRA more valuable over time, since taxes are never withheld or paid when a distribution occurs.

Estate Tax Benefit

A simple but significant benefit in the context of an estate is that a Roth IRA can effectively reduce estate taxes since the account contributions are made with post-tax dollars, thus reducing the size of your taxable estate. Always consult with an estate tax expert for guidance on your specific situation.

Roth IRA Disadvantages

Tax Deductibility

Contributions to a Roth IRA are not tax deductible whereas contributions to a traditional IRA are immediately tax deductible.

Reducing Adjusted Gross Income (AGI)

Without the benefit of tax deductibility, Roth IRA owners are not able to reduce their adjusted gross income (AGI). This disadvantage may be relevant to an owner who is at or near qualifying thresholds for various tax credits, or can use the tax deduction available when making annual contributions to all other type of IRA accounts.

Eligibility + Income Limits

Not all investors are eligible to contribute to a Roth IRA. Contributions are limited based on income earned. Alternatively, employer-sponsored plans including 401(k), 403(b), Simple IRA or SEP IRA plans offer both immediate tax deductibility and often times much higher income limits.

Bracketology - Watch Your Tax Bracket

If you consistently fall into the high tax brackets, Roth IRA owners are likely to pay more income tax on their earnings that are then contributed into the Roth IRA. For example: if your combined State and Federal tax rate is 35%, you need to earn $6,750.00 to have $5,000 in after-tax dollars for a Roth IRA contribution.

Retirement and State Income Taxes

In which state do you plan to retire? Where do you live now? If you currently live in a state that imposes income tax but plan to retire in a state free of income tax (or one with a lower rate), Roth IRA contributions may be a disadvantage. This is because you will pay state income taxes before you make the contribution and thus not benefit from the tax-free withdrawal if your state of residence in retirement has lower or no state income tax.

Rule Changes

It happens in sports, it happens in Congress - future rule changes may alter the playing field as it relates to tax-free withdrawal benefits for Roth IRA accounts. It is possible that in the future Congress may decide to erode the tax-free status of earnings within a Roth IRA. Many who have studied the possibility of rule changes of the Roth IRA feel only those accounts established after new rules go into effect would be impacted. However, as more investors take advantage of the Roth IRA vehicle, there will be those in Congress who target these funds as a source of income for continued government spending programs.

Plans for the Self-Employed

Savings Incentive Match Plan for Employees (SIMPLE)

SIMPLE, short for Savings Incentive Match Plan for Employees, is structured as an incentive-match plan for small businesses with fewer than 100 employees. It is well suited to business owners who pay themselves less than $45,000 per year in wages.

The employee's contribution is made via salary deferral with contributions limited to $11,500 per year, increasing to $14,000 per year if you are 50 years of age or older. Employers add a percentage of the employee's contributions in the form of a match, of up to three percent each year.

For real estate investors, small business owners or sole proprietors who wish to make larger contributions and receive larger tax deductions, the SIMPLE can be a very effective choice. It can also be used for your spouse and children as long as they are employees of the company and meet minimum income requirements.

Before getting started, it's important to look at the eligibility rules:
- Business must have fewer than 100 employees
- Participating employees must earn at least $5,000 of income in the calendar year
- Employees must earn the minimum amount specified by the employer during the two preceding years

Standard withdrawal rules and penalties apply to the SIMPLE IRA:
- Withdrawals can begin at age 59½
- Withdrawals taken before age 59½ incur a 10% penalty
- Withdrawals taken before age 59½ on an account which is less than 2 years old may incur a higher penalty
- Required minimum distributions begin at age 70½
- All withdrawals and minimum distributions are taxed as ordinary income

Simplified Employee Pension (SEP IRA)

The Simplified Employee Pension (SEP IRA) is similar to the SIMPLE IRA. SEP IRAs are suited to small businesses providing a low-cost plan suitable for both owner-operated businesses and those with a small number of employees.

SEP IRA funds are treated in the same manner as traditional IRAs, providing tax deductions on the initial contribution with income taxes payable upon withdrawal.

Eligibility rules and contribution limits are as follows:

- Businesses which have at least one employee are eligible regardless of their structure (corporation, partnership or sole proprietorship)
- Employees must be at least 21 years of age, have worked for the business during any 3 of the previous 5 years and earned at least $550 in income (by 2012 IRS rules)
- Spouse and children are eligible as long as they are employees of the company and meet minimum income requirements
- The total contribution cannot exceed the lesser of 25% of an employee's income or $50,000 in 2012
- The maximum income to be eligible is $250,000 in 2012
- All employees must receive the same contribution percentage. Therefore, as an owner-employee, you cannot contribute more by percentage to your SEP IRA than you contribute to your employees' plans
- The deadline for establishing and contributing to the SEP plan is the tax-filing deadline of the business plus any approved extensions

Standard withdrawal rules and penalties apply:
- Withdrawals can begin at age 59½
- Withdrawals taken before age 59½ incur a 10% penalty
- Withdrawals taken before age 59½ on an account which is less than 2 years old may incur a higher penalty

- Required minimum distributions begin at age 70½
- All withdrawals and minimum distributions are taxed as ordinary income

In the context of SEP IRA contributions, net compensation for self-employed individuals is generally the net profit from IRS Schedule C minus one-half of the individual's self-employment tax. Speak with your tax advisor to determine which plan is most advantageous to you.

Individual-K or Solo 401(k) Plans

The Individual Solo 401(k) combines some of the best attributes from the SIMPLE and SEP plans. This plan is suitable for self-employed individuals, where the owner(s) and their spouses are the only plan members. Account holders have the benefit of making high contributions and receiving potentially large tax deductions while also benefiting from an employer profit-sharing contribution.

Eligibility rules and contribution limits are as follows:

- Plan must be established by the last day of your business tax year
- Each owner working in the business may contribute via salary deferral up to 100% of income or $17,000 (whichever is less) increasing to $22,500 annually if you are over 50 years of age
- The annual compensation cap is $250,000 for 2012
- Profit-sharing contributions are limited to 25% of income for a corporation or 20% of self-employment income for a sole proprietorship or partnership, up to the annual compensation
- The combined contribution limit is $50,000 annually, increasing to $55,500 if you are 50 years of age or older
- This must be the only plan maintained by the business

Standard withdrawal rules and penalties apply:
- Withdrawals can begin at age 59½

- Withdrawals taken before age 59½ incur a 10% penalty
- Withdrawals taken before age 59½ on an account which is less than 2 years old may incur a higher penalty
- Required minimum distributions begin at age 70½
- All withdrawals and minimum distributions are taxed as ordinary income

Roth Individual-(k) or Roth Solo 401(k)

The Roth Solo 401(k) plan offers the same benefits as the Individual Solo 401(k) plan detailed above, however, as the name suggests, a Roth 401(k) combines features of the traditional 401(k) with those of the Roth IRA. It's offered by employers like a regular 401(k) plan, but as with a Roth IRA, contributions are made with after-tax dollars.

While you don't get an upfront tax-deduction, the account grows tax-free, and withdrawals taken during retirement aren't subject to income tax, provided you're at least 59 1/2 when you begin withdrawals and you've held the account for five years or more.

The Roth 401(k) can offer advantages to high-income individuals who haven't been able to contribute to a Roth IRA in the past because of the income restrictions.

What plan is best for me?

Most financial experts agree that tax rates in the not-too-distant future will need to increase in order to support Government spending, while the deductions most high earners have counted on in the past are being slowly eliminated. With a little study of the retirement plan options available, along with sound advice from your tax professional or your custodian, you will find the plan that fits your needs and be on your way to building an account you can manage with ease.

The only possible bad choice is to not take advantage of the above options that allow you to keep the profits you earn without having to share them each year with the tax man.

Chapter 3.1

HOW DO I GET MORE MONEY INTO MY SELF DIRECTED RETIREMENT PLAN?

Your Annual contribution limits

Generally, there are two ways to go about getting funds into your retirement plan. As the account owner, you may (1) make an annual contribution (deposit) into your retirement plan, taking into account the limitations established by the IRS or you can (2) transfer funds from an existing account (IRA, 401(k), 403-(b), etc) into the self-directed IRA.

Since the creation of the IRA back in 1974, the majority of the rule changes issued by the IRS have been related to the amount of funds we can annually deposit into our retirement plans. Because of the frequency of rule changes surrounding contribution limits, you should check with your tax adviser, your custodian or the Internal Revenue Service website (www.irs.gov) for more information on the annual contribution limits for the type of account(s) you have.

Contributions

Back in Chapter 3.0 you'll find a chart that describes each type of retirement plan with the annual contribution limits. It's important to know that regardless of how many retirement plans you participate in or the type of accounts (IRAs, 401(k)'s, etc) you have, the IRS has imposed a limit on the total amount of money you can deposit into your retirement plan basket each year.

Rollovers-Transfers from existing plans

When it comes to transferring assets to a self-directed IRA, you can do so from any other type of IRA or 401(k) plan. As the IRA account owner, you are free to transfer your funds into another IRA type account whenever you wish. When it comes to 401(k) plans you'll often have restrictions based on whether you are currently employed by the company that provided the account as an employee benefit.

It is prudent to note that you can rollover or transfer funds from one account to another tax-free. Rollovers refer to the distribution of cash or other assets from one retirement plan to another. The only exception is if you are dealing with a return on an excess contribution or a required distribution. To make the rollover, you can either request the funds be transferred directly to an account or have the funds paid to you and then have them transferred within 60 days to a new account. Your custodian will help you avoid any penalty when you initiate a rollover or transfer of funds to a new account.

If you have an eligible rollover distribution paid to you, the payer must withhold 20% of the amount transferred to comply with the rules of federal tax withholding. You would therefore receive only 80% of the distribution. To avoid this taxation, you can roll the funds directly to an IRA or an eligible retirement plan. Rollovers are not tax deductible, and rollover distributions must be reported on your tax return. Rollovers must also be made within 60 days from receipt of the distribution unless the IRS extends the time limit in acknowledgement that there are factors beyond your control affecting your ability to comply with the time limit. If you want to avoid taxes on the entire amount, 100% of the distribution must be rolled over. It is important to note that you can roll over assets in kind. Real property is one example of an asset in kind.

Often the most challenging aspect of opening a self-directed retirement account is the timing. Many investors, upon learning about the benefits of a self-directed retirement plan, shop for property before they establish and fund their accounts. Save everyone some frustration by getting your account established before you begin looking at investments. What often happens is that an investor finds a great deal from a very motivated seller who needs a fast escrow closing to solve underlying problems. The seller or real estate agent pushes to close the deal, and if you, the buyer, have not opened and funded your account, the seller may move on when you are unprepared to close. This is by far the most common mistake I see IRA investors make. Be sure you can live up to any offer to purchase. Never assume a quick or timely transfer of funds between your existing custodian and your new custodian; it is out of your control.

A transfer can take several days to a full month, depending on the type of assets and the capabilities of the institutions involved. Cash transfers can take up to 30 days while the transfer of other asset types can take as much as 60 days to complete. If you are rolling assets, such as real estate holdings and deeds of trust, from a qualified plan, be prepared for the transaction to take up to two months.

One way to avoid this time frame for transfers is to roll assets directly and then establish them in your new account within the 60-day period mandated by law. The institution to which you are transferring the assets will generally be happy to provide you with the necessary forms to initiate the transaction.

Chapter 3.2

WHAT CAN I OWN IN MY IRA?

Although this book is primarily focused on owning real, tangible assets such as real estate in the retirement plan, you are not limited to holding only hard assets in the self-directed IRA. The same assortment of publicly-traded securities that has traditionally been held in a retirement plan is always available to you as the account holder, including:

- Stocks
- Bonds
- Mutual funds
- ETFs
- Money market funds
- Put and call options
- Certificates of deposit

In the non-publicly-traded category of assets that can be owned in the self directed retirement plan you'll find:

- Real estate
- Mortgages and deeds of trust
- Private notes
- Tax liens
- Options to purchase real estate
- Precious metals that are considered non-collectible
- Private stock
- Limited partnerships in real estate, oil and gas, equipment leasing and agriculture
- Venture capital

The list of possible investments is actually so extensive it's easier to think in terms of, "What can I *not* own in my retirement plan?" which is covered in Chapter 3.3. The way the rules on retirement plan investing are written, there are only three areas you'll need to avoid:

1. Life insurance
2. Collectibles
3. Stock in a Subchapter S corporation

Real Estate for the Retirement Plan

In Chapter 8 we'll cover each type of real estate you may wish to explore owning as well as touch on the advantages and disadvantages to consider when making your investment decisions. For now, here is a list to get you thinking about various investing options when considering real estate:

- Single-family houses
- Multi-family houses
- Vacation property
- Land
- Commercial buildings
- Office buildings
- Shopping centers
- Self- storage facilities
- Campgrounds / marinas
- Farmland / orchards / ranches
- Foreign real estate
- Mortgages and deeds of trust
- Tax liens and tax certificates

On many of the above types of real estate, you can apply different methods or investing strategies of generating profits, all of which flow back into the retirement plan without being taxed upon receipt. The ability to make either short or long-term profits without paying a tax on the gain is what makes investing with your retirement plan so attractive. As the old saying goes, "It's not what you make but what you keep that counts."

In many cases, you can deploy more than one profit strategy on the same property, either simultaneously or by shifting strategies over time as changes in the local real estate market occur.

The intent of this book is to share some of the more basic and popular real estate investing strategies. There are countless books on the market that can teach you the so-called secrets to building wealth with real estate. Many of my favorites are listed in the **Additional Resources** section of this book.

Common Real Estate Investing Strategies

Buy and hold
Buy and rent
Buy, fix and flip (sell)
Buy, fix and rent
Build and sell
Build and rent
Buy and sell at wholesale
Buy and change the use (commercial to residential or residential to commercial)
Sell as "rent to own"
Sell with "seller financing"
Sandwich lease
Land development
Buying/selling options to purchase property

Chapter 3.3

WHAT ASSETS CAN I NOT OWN IN MY IRA?

There are many types of investments and assets you can hold in an IRA. The list of allowable investments seams to grow each year, as investors get more and more creative. Again, the overriding theme for many self-directed investors is "invest in what you know," so you'll be amazed at what creative investors own in their retirement plans. I'll share some interesting stories a little later that you will most likely be sharing with your investing friends.

Let's take a look at the areas in which you are <u>Not Allowed</u> to invest your retirement funds.

Life Insurance

Life insurance contracts are prohibited from being held in the retirement plan. The life insurance industry and those who provide advice on the best ways to use life insurance are by far some of the most creative financial engineers in the world today. I encourage you to research the many benefits of using trusts, family partnerships and estate planning tools available. Just don't buy life insurance in your IRA. Any competent insurance professional will stop you from making this mistake by refusing to issue the policy to your retirement plan.

Collectibles

The other type of asset you cannot purchase in a retirement plan is anything considered a collectible. The Internal Revenue Code specifically lists the following assets as collectibles:

- Works of art
- Antique furnishings and rugs
- Stamps
- Gemstones

- Alcoholic beverages
- Numismatic coins

The IRA custodian industry has had so many questions on what is and is not considered a collectible that you'll find many custodians have added certain assets to the list that they consider collectibles and therefore will not allow a client's account to hold. These additional assets include:

- Rare books or magazines
- Antique automobiles and aircraft
- Firearms
- Historic documents
- Sports memorabilia

And just about anything else that has value derived from its scarcity.

As you can imagine, there is often a difference of opinion over what should or shouldn't be a collectible. Gold, silver and platinum coins have been very good investments over the last 10 or more years, and many investors want to hold precious metals in their retirement plans. Certain coins are minted in limited quantities so what today may be a common coin may become a collectible tomorrow. Custodians who are willing to allow accounts to hold precious metals will describe the type of coins and bullion you can own. They can also talk with you about which precious metals dealers they have the most experience working with. At the end of the day, the custodian you choose will clearly disclose their own rules on what you can and cannot purchase with your retirement plan.

If you plan on owning anything in your IRA that may be considered a collectible, speak with your custodian and insist on receiving a copy of the rules enforced on client accounts.

Making a mistake in this area by buying assets that are deemed to be collectibles can carry a substantial IRS penalty. The amount invested into the collectible asset is considered a distribution from the account to you in the year you made the purchase, and if you are under age 59 1/2, you may be required to pay the 10% early-distribution penalty.

Chapter 4.0

ESTABLISHING A SELF-DIRECTED IRA OR 401(K) PLAN

When you are ready to use your retirement plan to make a real estate purchase, or any other type of alternative investment, you'll need to open a self-directed retirement account.

For IRAs, the custodian or trustee is normally either a bank or trust company. Insurance companies and other entities approved by the Secretary of the Treasury to carry out the responsibilities of a custodian or trustee of individual retirement accounts may also serve as your custodian. Custodians are ultimately regulated by state or federal agencies. All of the custodians we recommend hold account funds at depository banks so their deposits of cash are insured by the Federal Deposit Insurance Corporation (FDIC). If the bank used by your custodian is a non-depository bank, its regulator may require the placement of un-invested cash deposits into FDIC-insured instruments.

It has become popular for financial institutions to label the retirement plans they offer as self-directed.

Discount brokerage firms like Fidelity and Schwab, offer their clients self-directed accounts. However, the client is still limited to the investment products offered by these firms which, again, are stocks, bonds and mutual funds; most investors are looking to diversify away from these business-as-usual investments. Insurance companies typically take the same path, offering insurance-related products to their clients, although the trend is to offer a family of mutual funds managed by an affiliated company.

A truly self-directed account allows all of the brokerage firm/insurance company products *in addition* to alternative investments into real estate, mortgages, precious metals, tax liens, etc.

The most successful investors I know have several retirement plans, and they keep their Wall Street investments in their discount -brokerage IRA, their insurance company investments at their insurance company retirement plan and their alternative investments with a purely self-directed IRA custodian.

I have had several clients ask their CPAs to become their custodians. This has never worked, primarily because of the lengthy approval process required to become a custodian and the necessity to meet state and federal requirements. Save yourself some time and select the services from a custodian well-established in the retirement plan business. Even larger CPA firms are not going to have enough clients to justify the efforts required to become a custodian.

If you are planning to own real estate in your IRA, knowledge of the account rules and investment authorization process created by your custodian, are important to understand in order to achieve an easy transaction. For the purpose of making your first self directed investment, it helps to initially select a custodian who offers some form of education to you on their procedures. It typically takes less than 20 minutes to learn the steps your custodian requires you to take when buying real estate with your self directed account.

To select a custodian with the lowest annual fees, you may need to establish an out-of-state account, depending on where you live. These days, the largest custodians offer educational events online that are easy to attend if you do select a firm located outside your area.

When selecting a custodian, look closely at the *team* you are hiring. For example, is there a tax attorney or CPA on staff to answer the more complex questions you or your tax professionals may have? Do the principals have experience in the type of industry's you may decide to invest in? Does the custodian have a specialized focus, i.e. precious metals, or do they allow you to own all types of assets? Chapter 4.1 provides a list of the custodians we suggest you research. Keep in mind that custodians are prohibited from making investment recommendations to their clients, so don't expect them to suggest specific opportunities to you as a client.

Your custodian, administrator or trustee must provide you with a written IRA custodial trustee account disclosure and service agreement. This document will outline the features of the plan; pay particular attention to it to ensure that you have the features you need. Specifically, you should make certain that you are allowed to select real estate, precious metals, etc before you open the account.

An IRA is a depository account that can be established only by an individual. All activity is done in the name of the trustee or custodian for the benefit of (FBO) the account owner.

To open an IRA, note the following:

- All IRA applications will be undertaken in your name. It is your personal name that is required and cannot be the name of your spouse or the name of any trust or company you may own in whole or in part.

- You will need to give your address and social security number to open an account.

- In some instances, an Employer Identification Number (EIN) is required while SEP IRAs require the name of an employer.

- You must specify the type of account you want to own.

- Be prepared to establish who you will designate as your beneficiary. Designation may not be required when you open the account, but it is strongly encouraged.

To open a 401(k) plan, note the following:
- If you are an employer or self-employed with no other employees, you may be able to act as the trustee for your qualified plan. Qualified plans, unlike IRAs, are not subject to a mandate with regard to banks or institutions fulfilling the role of trustee or custodian.

- With a qualified plan, you may select as trustee yourself, another individual or group of individuals, a corporation, or a combination of these parties. When you establish a qualified plan, however, you may need to verify that the plan is self-directed by playing close attention to the investment section of your plan document. You will need to fill out an adoption agreement associated with your plan document. This agreement will contain all of the information regarding the operations of the plan, including details for terms of eligibility, vesting, contributing and allocations.

If you are an employer, you can use an IRS-approved prototype or master plan to establish your qualified plan. These are offered by sponsoring organizations.

Alternatively, you can prepare and adopt your own written plan so long as it satisfies the qualification requirements of the IRS Code. An experienced retirement plan advisor is the best person to consult in this regard.

The plan, whether you develop it yourself or base it on a prototype or master plan, must be in writing and detailed to your employees, with the provisions stated clearly in the document.

The plan must also be exclusively for the benefit of employees and their beneficiaries. Hence, all should be allowed to participate in the plan so long as they are at least 21 years of age and have been employed by your company for a specified period of time.

As an employer, you will be required to use the same taxpayer ID for the plan that you used on the adoption agreement. You, or another person or entity designated by you, will serve as the trustee, custodian or administrator as per the adoption agreement.

One final point to make, regarding the establishment of a new self directed retirement plan. The custodian you select will be able to answer your questions on the amount of time it will require to create your account and complete the transfer of assets. At certain times of the year, around April 15th and in late December when processing year-end transactions, custodians are often flooded with new accounts. If possible try to avoid these periods if you are want a quick and easy transaction.

It is also important to have the help of an experienced advisor when it comes to making your first transaction. After making a few investments in the retirement plan, you'll find the entire process is very simple.

The one comment I hear from clients at the end of their first transaction is how surprisingly easy the process was. A good custodian will have made the forms easy and self-explanatory. In an effort to compete effectively, many custodians are now offering to do most of the paperwork for you. Just give them the basic transactions forms, such as the purchase agreement for a property, and they will complete everything you need to sign as the account owner and overnight it to you for signature. In a few days, the property you've selected will be owned by the retirement plan, and you are on your way to earning more tax-free or tax-deferred wealth.

Chapter 4.1

ESTABLISHING YOUR SELF-DIRECTED IRA

Your first step into the world of self-directed retirement plans is to review the companies that will provide this unique but fast-growing service. You'll discover two types of service providers:

Administrators

- Guide you in selecting the most appropriate type of retirement plan
- Guide you in selecting a custodian or Trust Company firm for your account
- Help you open the account and transfer funds from old accounts into your new account
- Provide educational information
- Assist in completing transactions
- Provide statements to the account owner
- Report account values to the IRS and the account holder each year
- Deposit your funds into an FDIC-insured bank
- Charge an annual fee, as well as transaction fees
- Do not make investment recommendations
- Occasionally provide networking events for clients
- <u>Are not custodians or trust companies,</u> which are more closely regulated

Custodians

- Guide you in selecting the most appropriate type of retirement plan
- Help you open the account and transfer old accounts into your new account
- Provide educational information
- Assist in completing transactions
- Provide statements to the account owner
- Report account values to the IRS and the account holder each year
- Deposit your funds into an FDIC-insured bank
- Charge an annual fee, as well as transaction fees
- Do not make investment recommendations
- Occasionally provide networking events for clients
- <u>Are regulated by banking laws and/or the IRS</u>

I recommend getting on the email list for several of the industry's top-rated administrators and custodians. Since service fees vary little between these firms, you will find that they tend to compete by providing educational services on their web sites, via seminars or with various online events. These firms make it easy to learn the rules as well as navigate through all the investment opportunities that fit well into your retirement account.

Below is a list of the Self Directed IRA Custodians many investors use.

IRA Custodian List

New Direction IRA, Inc.
1070 W. Century Drive, STE-101
Louisville, CO 80027
Phone: 877.742.1270
http://www.newdirectionira.com/

The IRA Club
Dennis Blitz, President
79 W Monroe
Suite 1208 Chicago, IL 60603-4936
Phone: 888.795-7950
http://www.iraclub.org/

Horizon Trust Company
4801 Lang NW, Suite-110
Albuquerque, NM
Phone: 888.205.6036
http://www.HorizonTrust.com

Equity Trust
225 Burns Road
Elyria, OH 44035
Phone: 888.382.4727
http://www.trustetc.com/

Summit Trust Company
8861 West Sahara Ave, STE-215
Las Vegas, NV 89117
Phone: 877.268.9115
http://www.summittrust.com

Chapter 4.2

HOW DO I KNOW THE CUSTODIAN WON'T RIP ME OFF?

Although there is always a possibility of fraud when someone has access to your investment funds, even when they are deposited in your local bank, all custodians are either owned by or affiliated with a bank that has FDIC insurance for all accounts up to the current limit of $250,000. If you are concerned about the integrity of the custodian you are about to open an account with, ask for authorizing documentation from the state or federal banking regulators. The Better Business Bureau will often have a rating on the custodian firm, and if the level of customer service has been less than satisfactory, you will see complaints from past customers, just like you would on a bank that lacks sufficient service.

I often remind clients that the large majority of the assets in their self-directed retirement plans are going to consist of hard assets like real estate, precious metals or shares in a private company in which they choose to invest. Even if the custodian were to go out of business or defraud clients, the assets would not be easily stolen from your account.

But what if the unthinkable did happen? Let's say the custodian went out of business from fraud or just poor management. If you own real estate in the retirement account, the real estate is still there. Title to the property cannot be transferred to someone else's name without your signature as the account owner. Sure, you would have some forms to complete that would transfer the title of the property to a new custodian, but the loss of your retirement funds would not turn into a Bernie Madoff type fiasco because the assets are real, tangible assets.

I've never heard of a custodian firm being charged with fraud. Keep in mind these are trust companies which simply hold account assets for their clients. They do not make mortgage or business loans like a bank, or trade in risky derivative markets. When I do run across a self-directed account owner who is unhappy, it always comes down to either lack of service or the fees charged by the custodian. These types of service problems can always be fixed by moving your account to a new custodian, just like you have most likely done when your local bank failed to provide good service.

The majority of the larger self-directed custodians offer the ability to open and maintain a discount brokerage account within the self-directed retirement plan. You always have access to the financial market to diversify your investments into liquid markets. For many self-directed investors, their brokerage account (held in the name of their custodian account) will be used to invest in more liquid assets while they shop for their next real estate opportunity.

Self-directed custodian firms have had to make a large financial investment (approximately $500,000) and endure months of red tape to receive the regulatory approval required to offer their services. Although this doesn't guarantee they will always provide great customer service, it does mean that not everyone can launch a new custodian business from a spare bedroom they've just converted to an office.

Chapter 4.3

I WANT TO USE MY LOCAL BANK OR CPA AS MY CUSTODIAN

Many investors just beginning their research into self-directed retirement plans are often frustrated when they learn that they cannot use their local bank or even a good friend who happens to be a CPA as their self-directed custodian.

The common reasons your local bank will not offer a Self-directed IRA account are:

- They are not equipped or staffed to pay all the monthly property bills related to owning real estate

- They don't make commissions when you buy or sell real estate or precious metals

- They have not satisfied banking regulations to be a trust company

- They don't want the responsibility of monitoring IRS regulations

- They are prohibited from being your custodian if they have a business relationship with you; that rules out your accountant as an option

Most local banks and accounting firms just don't have enough local demand for these services to establish a special department to properly service these self-directed accounts, nor can they justify the start-up expenses to become a trust company.

If you insist on keeping your retirement funds in a local bank read Chapter 6 on Checkbook IRA Accounts and Chapter 3 on Solo-401(k) accounts.

Both of these types of accounts give you the ability to select where your funds are deposited. The checkbook IRA (an industry term, not an IRS term) allows you to administer the accounting tasks, including opening a bank account and writing checks as well as making deposits. These accounts still require the use of a custodian, although the custodian's role is dramatically reduced to providing annual valuation reports to the IRS as well as the account owner.

For a list of who I consider to be today's top custodians, see Chapter 4.1 or visit: www.IRAassets.com If you are a first-time visitor to the site, you will need to register and then type the word "custodian" into the search box.

Chapter 4.4

HOW TO MINIMIZE FEES CHARGED TO YOUR SELF DIRECTED RETIREMENT ACCOUNT

Of course no one enjoys paying fees, but when you compare the annual fees required to maintain a self-directed retirement plan against the taxes you will have saved, you'll be far ahead of the retirement game with a self-directed IRA.

Here are several steps you can take to reduce fees:

- Plan your transaction in advance – manage the expectations of seller, lender and real estate agents in the deal by agreeing to a realistic escrow closing date
- If you hold real estate in your IRA, pay any monthly recurring fees on an annual basis by making a deposit to the utility companies against which they can bill
- If you use property managers for real estate investments, request them to pay all expenses and credit your IRA with the net proceeds from the property each month
- Avoid "rush delivery" of payments sent by your custodian
- Request discounts from the custodian if you have several accounts
- Ask your custodian for referral fees if you send friends who open accounts
- Complete many of your custodian transactions online
- Go paperless vs. mailed statements
- Be aware of the minimum account balance requirements and associated penalties

The self-directed retirement plan business is growing more competitive each year. Custodians have been known to invest as much as $500 to attract each new client who opens a new account. Ask your custodian for discounts and ideas on how to save on both annual as well as transaction fees.

Keep in mind, as is the case with many services we buy, you get what you pay for in the self-directed retirement plan industry. I've found that the lower the fee, the less customer service you'll receive.

At the end of the day, of course custodians want you to be successful so you'll refer others to the self-directed method of retirement plan investing.

Chapter 5

TRANSFERS FROM A 401K TO AN IRA

It's easy to transfer a 401(k) account from a past employer into a self-directed IRA. For many people you may *have* to move your 401(k) savings if you are no longer employed by that employer.

There is no good reason to retain a 401(k) if you no longer work for a particular company; in fact, it's dangerous to leave money in a plan you can't control, or regularly monitor. Fees can be higher and investment choices are fewer. Companies amend their 401(k) plans often, since the rules applicable to these accounts are generated by the Department of Labor, and change often. Politicians like to meddle with retirement plans, resulting in unseen risks. Most employees don't read their 401(k) plan documents while employed, so it's very likely they won't read about the ongoing changes after they move into new employment or retire.

United Airlines Bankruptcy –

In 2002 United Airlines filed for Chapter 11 bankruptcy. Pilots and many others with pensions lost money and benefits. The Pension Benefit Guaranty Corporation took over the retirement plans, but federal regulations limited the amount of pension payments it would make to a maximum of about $45,000 a year. Many employees in the airline industry, which has been prone to bankruptcy, have learned to sweep company-provided retirement funds into a self-directed IRA whenever they are given the opportunity.

As a career commercial airline pilot, Peter has worked for a total of three large airlines; by the time he retired, he had spent the majority of his career with United Airlines. Each time the airline employing him merged with a stronger airline, he was given the option to either roll over his 401(k) into the new employer's 401(k) plan or transfer the funds into an IRA. Peter did what most of his fellow pilots elected to do which was to simply deposit his retirement savings into the new plan.

Looking back on his decision, Peter would tell you that the option to move those funds into an IRA was not made *obvious* as an alternative. Since 401(k) plan administrators (who are often the authors of the documents handed to employees) seldom want to see funds leave their control, they just make it super easy to transfer funds from the old plan into the new plan. After retiring, Peter had another choice on the management of his 401(k). He could leave it with United or do a rollover to an IRA. Again, Peter followed what most other retiring pilots did that year; he left the funds in the 401(k) and began enjoying his retirement. Everything was fine until United Airlines filed for bankruptcy and Peter's large pension plan was frozen. After several years, a federal bankruptcy judge ruled that United Airlines would not be required to continue the pension plan on which Peter and so many other pilots relied. Peter would tell you today that he should have elected to move any 401(k) plan funds into an IRA immediately after his employment changed or when he ultimately retired.

Let's face it, changing jobs can be a stressful experience, especially when you don't have control over the timing of that change. It's natural to procrastinate on the transfer of your 401(k) plan into an IRA, especially when other options offered are custom- tailored to keep your funds under the control of others. Unless you have a strong aversion to managing and controlling your own future retirement success, I urge you to consider sweeping all 401(k) plans provided by past employers into an IRA you control.

Again no one cares more about your money than you do. Even if you are not ready to go the 100% self-directed route, at least move 401(k) funds out of the company plan and into a discount brokerage account that you control.

There has been plenty of news recently about underfunded pension plans in the majority of the states. If you are counting on a pension plan to help fund your retirement, you are at risk of being told the promises made to you by former elected officials just can't be kept and that you'll be paid less than you expected. The sad reality is that many who have been counting on their pension plan to provide a safe retirement just won't get what they have been expecting. If the option exists, consider taking a lump-sum distribution from your pension plan if it is under-funded, and moving your savings into an IRA to avoid immediate tax on the distribution amount.

Chapter 5.1

THE IN-SERVICE ROLLOVER

What if all My Retirement Funds are in my Current Employer's 401(k) plan?

Many investors I hear from have just discovered this hidden world of self-directed IRA accounts and are excited by all the benefits of gaining control of their funds. Often in their initial research, they are faced with the apparent limitations on transferring their funds from their current employer 401(k) plan into their own self-directed IRA. Fortunately for many, there is a growing trend among larger companies to offer what is commonly called the "in-service rollover" option. Be prepared to read deep into your 401(k) plan document to discover a rarely-promoted option that you as a plan participant can exercise.

The Secrets of "In-service Rollovers"

Let me start by saying there is nothing more exciting about retirement plans than discovering you have the right to transfer a percentage of your savings from your company's 401(k) into an IRA and still remain an employee, eligible to receive on-going retirement benefits. Although often buried in fine print, this right is spelled out during the drafting of a company's 401(k) document or is subsequently included in an amendment to the plan documents. While these "in-service rollover" provisions are more commonly found in plan documents at larger Fortune 500 or publicly-traded companies, that's not to say you won't find this option in smaller company plans, because it is becoming more and more common.

It's difficult to trace where this idea originated, however, I suspect that once-upon-a-time there was a savvy CFO with a large 401(k) plan balance and knowledge of being allowed to manage his own self-directed IRA. When the 401(k) plan administrator announced it was time to once again update the plan provisions, the CFO said, "Let's add a provision that permits employees to transfer a portion of their retirement funds from the 401(k) into their IRA account." My guess is that the idea was quickly shot down by the plan administrator as foolish or impossible since again, administrators typically resist the release of funds under their control. However, thanks to the persistence of that CFO many years ago, the plan administrator reluctantly agreed, and the "in-service rollover" was born.

How to Access Your 401K Funds Without Leaving Your Job

1. Your first step is to get a copy of your 401(k) plan document. This is a good idea even if you don't have your sites set on establishing a self-directed retirement plan. These plan documents are constantly being revised to comply with changes in the tax laws and Department of Labor regulations and far too often the changes are not to your benefit, so if you are counting on these funds during retirement, it's a good idea to know how the rules are changing. Depending on the size of the company that employs you, someone in Human Resources or Accounting can provide you with a copy of the plan document.

2. The Table of Contents of the plan document will typically direct you to the section on transfers or the rollover of your funds within the plan. Within that section, look for the words "in-service rollover" or "in-service transfers." Not every plan document will offer the "in-service rollover" option. If you are fortunate to have a plan with this option, don't be surprised to find some limitation on your ability to make transfers, or the percentage of your funds that can be moved to a vehicle under your control or how often you can exercise your transfer rights. If you are not so fortunate to find the option exists in your plan, don't give up! Speak with personnel in the Human Resources Department to see if they are aware of this type of transfer. It may be they have permitted transfers of this kind or have future plans to amend the plan by including the "in-service rollover" provision. If you work for a smaller company, enabling you to meet with the CFO or President, request the addition of the "in-service rollover" to the next plan revision. At the end of the

day, it is your money in the plan. With few exceptions, most CFOs welcome the suggested improvement to the 401(k) plan since they too want the best plan for their own benefit as well as everyone in the company.

3. If your plan permits an "in-service rollover," be prepared for resistance from the Human Resources Department or the plan administrator. Far too often, I get calls from clients who have discovered they have the right to transfer a portion of their 401(k) plan funds into an IRA but are told that it's not possible. In the majority of these cases, the "in-service" request has been posed to the wrong person or to someone without knowledge of the language in the plan document. In some cases, you'll be the first employee to actually make an "in-service rollover" request, so don't be surprised if you receive a look of confusion or reluctance to help with your transfer. Be prepared to point out the section of the plan document when you make your request. It's hard to argue with the black and white details printed in the plan document.

"Persistence Pays Big Dividends"

Phil had spent many years working for a large oil and gas company in Houston, Texas, when we first discussed self-directed IRA accounts. We discussed the opportunity to initiate an "in-service rollover" so he could buy land as a long-term investment. His company's 401(k) plan was administered by a well-known discount brokerage firm. Before calling to begin the transfer into his self-directed IRA, Phil did his homework and had a copy of his 401(k) plan in hand, which he'd highlighted to fully understand the limitations on his planned transfer.

When Phil called the administrator's toll-free service number, he encountered a young man who insisted he couldn't help Phil with the transfer. Obviously, the service representative had never been trained to handle this type of request. Or, on second thought, maybe his training was focused on deterring transfers; we'll never know. Regardless, when Phil spoke with a supervisor, he learned that the call center operators who typically help clients with stock trades and opening new accounts didn't have access to a copy of the 401(k) plan that Phil had in front of him. Phil's persistence paid off when he was able to complete his transfer by speaking to a specialist within the administrator's 401(k) department.

In helping many clients access their 401(k) funds over the last decade, I've learned a shortcut I want to share with you. If your plan administrator is a large brokerage firm like Fidelity or Charles Schwab and there is an "in-service rollover" provision in your plan, it is far easier to transfer your 401(k) funds into a new IRA account opened at that administrator's (brokerage) firm. If your ultimate goal is to fund a self-directed IRA that can hold real estate, precious metals or other assets you control, just follow these steps:

1. Open an IRA with the current administrator who now sends you your 401(k) statements. You will then have two retirement accounts at that firm, your 401(k) and a new IRA.
2. Request the "in-service rollover" from the 401(k) into the new IRA.
3. When the new IRA is funded, you can transfer any amount of funds you desire over to a self-directed IRA with the custodian of your choice.

The above steps may not seem like much of a shortcut at first glance, however, your 401(k) administrator perceives your transfer request as a "new account" when you open a new IRA with their firm. They like that since most brokerage firms pay bonuses to the employees who open new accounts. By opening a new IRA account, you'll begin to receive the service you deserve in order to complete your transfer to an IRA, as opposed to facing the resistance that too often occurs when the administrator senses you are pulling your funds out from under their control.

It's unfortunate that we as customers have to disguise our transfer this way, and I hope that will change in the future; however, I have found this method of transfer is much quicker than clearly communicating your plans to move your funds completely away from the 401(k) plan administrator.

Invest an hour of your time getting to know your 401(k) plan. As you read the documents ask yourself these questions:

- Can I transfer all or only a portion of this 401(k) into an IRA?
- How much can I as an employee deposit into the plan each year?
- How much does the employer contribute to the plan?
- How much can I borrow from the plan?
- If I'm in the hospital, unable to work, can my family access the 401(k) funds or borrow funds for an emergency?
- If my employer files bankruptcy or is acquired by a competitor, what happens to my plan?

Don't get caught off-guard by changes in the rules regardless of whether they come form the Department of Labor or your employer. The vast majority of investors generate far better annual investment results when they control their own retirement funds and invest in what they know.

Chapter 6

CHECKBOOK IRA ACCOUNTS

A penny saved is a penny earned.
~Benjamin Franklin

Checkbook IRA accounts are often the perfect solution for investors who actively manage their retirement plans. However you need to research and understand both the advantages as well as disadvantages of these accounts before selecting this option.

So what is a checkbook IRA account?

Put simply, it's a transaction management tool that allows the account holder to undertake many of the administration tasks associated with acquiring investments and managing the income and expenses associated with the investments you own within the retirement account.

Here's how it works. To start with, a self-directed IRA account is set up with a custodian, the same as any other self-directed IRA. Then, a "special purpose" limited liability company (LLC) is set up with you, the IRA owner named as the LLC manager. The custodian (after receiving written authorization from the IRA account owner) then transfers some or all of the IRA funds into the LLC as a purchase of LLC shares. That's right; your IRA is buying shares of the LLC you operate as an investment vehicle. The LLC manager proceeds to make investments and manage all associated administration (including depositing income and paying expenses), effectively using the "checkbook" to direct the investment funds, hence the name checkbook IRA. This type of account is marketed under various names including the checkbook LLC or Checkbook retirement plan.

There is often the initial misconception that using a checkbook IRA eliminates the requirement for a third-party custodian. It does not. However, it *does* drastically reduce the role of the custodian to that of a third-party reporting service. The IRS rules have always required that an independent third party report all contributions and withdrawals associated with these retirement plans, along with a year-end annual value of the account.

There are positives and negatives associated with these accounts, as well as the potential risk that the manager takes upon himself, instead of leveraging the expertise of the custodian in a self-directed IRA. The main advantage seen by users of the checkbook IRA is a reduction in custodian fees. Another advantage is that of accelerating transaction times, as the checkbook IRA owner does not have to wait for a custodian's processing time for a transaction. The checkbook IRA provides more freedom in truly managing a self-directed IRA, but with that freedom does come additional responsibilities which must be astutely managed.

Those who denounce the use of the checkbook IRA are predominantly risk- adverse individuals who highlight the benefits of having a trained professional custodian oversee all transactions passing through the self-directed IRA to ensure ongoing compliance with IRS Codes, as well as accurate and timely reporting.

Checkbook IRAs are a useful tool for the experienced investor who has the knowledge and means (i.e. time) to manage a self-directed IRA account within the provisions of the IRS Code. When executed well, this strategy may save a substantial amount of money in exchange for the time you invest, administering the funds in the retirement account. It also offers a more agile approach to investing, allowing owners to not only get in or out of investments quickly, but also allows an efficient means to manage the income and expenses associated with owning rental real estate.

For the less experienced investor or busy executive, checkbook IRAs can introduce a level of risk which may compromise the perceived benefits. Small errors in reporting or investment decisions are prosecuted aggressively by the IRS, and penalties can quickly erode savings or investment benefits. The decision to use a checkbook IRA account is entirely a personal assessment of your knowledge, available time and risk profile.

Know the true costs in advance

It's important to tally all the costs you'll incur as the owner of a checkbook IRA. An important component of establishing one of these accounts is the creation of a new Limited Liability Company (LLC) in the state of your choice. State fees to register a new LLC vary from as low as $100 to as much as $1,000. . The majority of the states also charge an annual fee for the privilege to conduct business. There are requirements to file annual reports with the Secretary of State and, of course, penalties for late filing.

In an attempt to operate your LLC in the most economical manner and save on fees, there is often some thought put into the best state in which to register your new business. It is my opinion that if the assets your LLC will own are located in the same state in which you reside, you have no choice over what state you should register your LLC in. It must be registered in your "home state" because that is clearly where you are doing business.

However, if you are doing business in a state while all of the assets of that business are located outside of your state of residency, some CPAs will be comfortable with you using the "out-of-state" LLC. This is clearly a question you must answer with the assistance of your own tax advisor.

It's important to keep in mind that when you form and operate an LLC, you are in fact operating a business, which requires a Federal Tax Identification number. This of course leads to the requirement to file a Federal Tax return with the IRS. For many investors, the preparation of an LLC tax return is an easy task; others will be wise to seek the assistance of a qualified tax preparer. Depending on the amount of business activity within your LLC each year, you may want to budget a few hundred dollars for the completion of the tax return.

There are many accounting software programs available today that make the record keeping for an LLC very simple. Quicken and QuickBooks are among the most popular while others have additional tools that incorporate real property management with the accounting task.

Although some investors are initially drawn to the ability to control the funds in their retirement plan by using a checkbook IRA, the real advantage is the potential to save on both the annual fees charged by the custodian and the transaction fees when an asset is purchased or sold by the IRA account.

An additional benefit can often be the ability to quickly purchase a new asset for the retirement plan or to pay a deposit fee when necessary. Investors who commonly buy property at auction will use the checkbook IRA since they can make the required payment on the day of the auction.

Chapter 6.1

CHECKBOOK IRAS MAKE AUCTION-BUYING EASY

Wade is an experienced building contractor in Las Vegas who has found good success when buying homes at the Clark County, Nevada, foreclosure auctions. I would put Wade in the Pro category when compared to the various types of self-directed IRA investors. After he completes all of his due diligence on a property scheduled for a foreclosure auction, he'll attend the auction event and bid against other buyers for purchase of the property deed or the mortgage that is secured by the property.

Since the auction rules require the winning bidder to make payment on the day of the auction with a cashiers check, Wade will visit his local bank in advance of the auction and purchase cashiers checks payable to the County Clerk or the auction house. He'll purchase several cashiers checks in various increments, so he can deliver full payment for any bid he wins that day at auction. If he is unsuccessful at the auction, he can deposit the cashiers checks back into his account or hold them for use at an upcoming auction in the near future.

Wade has found that using a checkbook IRA is the only way to easily and quickly be prepared for the frequent auctions in his market area. Even though most self-directed IRA custodians will be happy to prepare multiple cashiers checks, they typically charge a per-check fee and often need to ship the checks via overnight service which adds to the total costs to buy real estate at auction.

Investors focused on buying tax liens commonly use their checkbook IRAs because they can make payment on auction day, while reducing their custodian fees. Because tax liens are often purchased for relatively small amounts, the cost of paying a custodian transaction fee of $250 or more per deed can quickly eliminate the potential profits derived from holding a tax deed.

SECTION 3

Selecting the Right Investments for Your Retirement Plan

Chapter 7.0

SELF-DIRECTED INVESTMENT OPTIONS

Many of the investments held in Self-Directed IRA and 401(k) plans fall under the banner of what Wall Street likes to call "Alternative Investment Options." As you'll see in a moment, most of these asset classes have one thing in common: they don't trade on a national or international market and end the trading session with a new daily "Closing Price" like a stock, bond or mutual fund. So these assets are simply an alternative to the publicly-traded securities most often offered by Wall Street investment firms.

Many times, investors who are considering a Self-Directed Retirement plan will mistakenly assume that they cannot own the typical assortment of Wall Street securities in a Self-Directed account. Their fear is that if they self-direct their account, they may miss out on the next bull market in stocks or bonds, or they will be left entirely on their own without the constant flow of investment recommendations they now receive.

Rest assured that all of the large self-directed custodians in today's market will allow you to have a discount or even a full-service brokerage account within your self directed IRA or 401(k) plan. I'm often asked by new clients: "What happens to my cash reserves between investments or while I wait for the right opportunity to come along?" The answer is to establish a brokerage account in the name of your self-directed retirement plan so you can keep your capital working at all times. Transferring funds between the self-directed account and the brokerage account has become very easy with online banking or it can be done with a quick call to your custodian or brokerage firm.

For many investors who want to keep one foot in the alternative investment arena and the other in the Wall Street arena, the answer is to have two or more separate accounts, each with a specific role. Funds shift between the accounts depending on the best opportunities available at the time. Because of the benefit of having easy access to global market opportunities, I seldom advise clients to completely close an existing IRA held at a discount brokerage firm. You've done the hard work of opening the account; why not keep it if you like the brokerage firm, if for no other reason than to eliminate the task of completing the new account application. As an account holder with even a small balance, you gain access to much of the research and educational tools many of the best brokerage firm's offer.

In later chapters, we'll get into the details on all of the alternative investments you can own in the self-directed retirement plan, but here is a partial list of what you'll gain access to as a self-directed investor:

- **Real Estate**
- **Mortgages**
- **Precious Metals**
- **Promissory Notes**
- **Oil and Gas**
- **Private Business Ownership**
- **Alternative Energy**
- **Agriculture**
- **Venture Capital**
- **Private Equity**
- **Partnerships**
- **Non-collectible Hard Assets**

Many of the above asset classes can, of course, be obtained from a Wall Street brokerage firm in the form of mutual funds; however, your options are limited to what has been packaged for you, without the ability to shop for the best deal or to negotiate specific terms that fit your investment or retirement plan goals. For example, your ideal investment may be to own a rental home in your neighborhood. That's not the kind of asset your discount or full service stockbroker has the ability to offer.

In addition, you may have a friend with a great new idea that is sure to be a big hit in an industry you understand well. Becoming an early investor in a start-up business has its risks but at the same time, fortunes have been made by those who discover small companies who need growth capital and may be willing to sell you a stake in the business. Again, this type of opportunity of course isn't offered by your financial planner or stockbroker.

Owning alternative assets in a tax-advantaged account has made a huge difference in the retirement lifestyles of many self-directed investors. Most importantly, using a self-directed IRA or 401(k) plan allows you to invest in what you know and understand vs. just buying the mutual fund that did well in last year's market.

Chapter 7.1

YOUR INVESTMENT OPTIONS ARE ENDLESS

The meeting of preparation with opportunity generates the offspring we call luck.
~Tony Robbins

If you've read the section on the types of retirement plan accounts and now understand the role a custodian plays, it's time to consider all the investment options you have. One of the biggest problems I see investors make is procrastination over their decision to begin the self-directed approach to investing. They delay opening a self-directed account because they don't have an immediate opportunity to invest. In other words, they wait for the opportunity to land in their lap before they open the account and make an investment.

Ever hear the expression, "Leap and your wings will appear?" Experienced investors have learned that more money is lost to procrastination than any other factor. Good deals just don't stick around for a month while you rush to open your account, transfer funds and direct your custodian to write a check to make the investment you've located.

At the end of the day, the primary reasons to have a self-directed retirement plan are (1) to give you control over the investments you manage and (2) expand the type of assets that are held in your retirement account. If it's your desire to diversify your savings away from the standard Wall Street collection of paper assets and begin owning real, tangible assets you understand and control, then open your self-directed account, transfer a small amount of your savings into it and begin shopping for the right type of investment. You can always transfer additional funds from your older IRA or 401(k) plans after you find the perfect investment to hold in your account.

If you choose to go shopping for great opportunities *before* you have a self-directed account established, you may lose an opportunity to a competing investor who is able able to make a more attractive offer to the seller simply because he can pay the seller faster.

In a worst-case scenario you can always close your self-directed account and transfer your funds back to a brokerage account, if after shopping for the right opportunity; you don't find the right investment.

Invest in What You Know

We've covered this several times earlier in the book, however, I can't over-emphasize how important it is to invest your retirement savings into those assets or industries in which you have experience or knowledge. For generations, Wall Street has brainwashed us into believing that diversification is required for investment success and while I agree this is a good approach to reducing your risks, it is one of the biggest reasons most investors lose a portion of their capital every year. In an effort to diversify our portfolio, we end up owning assets we know very little about.

Learn From Your Past Mistakes

If you were to list your five largest investment losses, you would be in the company of many investors who incurred losses in industries in which they were not that familiar. And chances are, your biggest successes came from assets or industries with which you had familiarity. Remember, no one cares as much about your retirement savings as you do. Sure, there is more work and responsibility when you manage your own investments; but the opportunity for success is far greater when you have a higher level of control over your account and the capital you are managing.

Successful investing isn't a talent we are born with; it's a learned skill that comes from being a student of the market in which you are investing. This is one reason that so many investors have success in local real estate. They live in the market where they purchase property. They recognize a good bargain because they know what a property should be worth because they can compare it to what they know already own in that market.

Today's investor has so many tools to use when researching any type of market. With enough time and the right tools, you can become enough of a market expert and experience success if you apply the lessons available in the many investing books on the market or get the right coach to help you.

Asset Classes for the Self-Directed Retirement Plan

Let's take a look at the different types of assets that most self-directed investors hold in their retirement plan. In general, any investment you feel has the potential for a high level of profit is better to hold in a tax-advantaged account. In such an account, the taxes that would have otherwise been paid out in federal and state taxes remain under your control inside the retirement plan and help build your wealth. Chapter 2.2 covers how taxes can have a devastating effect on building long-term wealth. If taxes levied on investors increase, as many expect they must, putting more focus on sheltering profits from taxes becomes as important as selecting the right asset class to own.

At the same time if you want to roll the dice and take high risks on a penny stock or a venture capital type investment, consider doing so with non-retirement plan capital so if you do have a loss on the investment, you can take the loss and gain the tax benefits available. Your tax professional can provide guidance on the best way to acquire an asset based upon the probability of a loss occurring.

Many investors with self-directed retirement plans focus on not only holding assets they control in these accounts, but also those that fall into the alternative asset class. These are tangible or real asset investments like real estate, precious metals and equipment. In many instances, these assets are a good hedge against a decline in purchasing power of our currency.

In other words, as the value of the U.S. Dollar continues to decline, it takes more dollars to buy these same assets. In times of higher inflation, these assets become very popular as a way to counteract the loss in purchasing power our currency experiences. I personally believe we are entering another cycle of high inflation, not only in the United States but around the world, as the majority of countries pump extra capital into their economies in an attempt to revive economic growth.

Alternative Asset Classes

It is difficult to pinpoint the exact time that Wall Street began labeling investments as alternative assets, but we know these asset classes were used, for the most part, to generate wealth long before the trading of stocks became popular. If your experience in any of the areas listed below is of a basic nature only, I recommend doing a great deal of research and obtaining independent advice before making your initial investment. You'll find many good investment books written on how to analyze the opportunities in each of these industries.

These are the most common alternative assets held in self-directed retirement plans:

Real Estate

An entire section of this book is devoted to owning real estate in the retirement plan. Many of the reasons investors buy real estate outside of their retirement plan also apply to why they hold property *inside* their tax-advantaged accounts. Real estate investors often point out that the tax advantages of owning investment property are lost when the property is held in a retirement plan. It is true that the common tax benefits of depreciation are lost whenever the property is held in a tax-advantaged account; however, many investors who buy property to get the early-stage tax benefits experience a rude awakening when they sell the investment property and are required to recapture all of the annual depreciation benefits at the time of sale.

If you look at the total after-tax profits of owning real estate in a retirement plan compared to owning the property outside of a tax-advantaged account, the net returns are almost always higher. In Chapter 9 we cover more on the topic of taxes and the dangers of completing real estate exchanges,(often called 1031 exchanges) in order to delay tax payments into the future.

Precious Metals

Gold, silver and platinum are typically good inflation-hedge assets to hold in self-directed retirement plans. Most custodians require a third-party depositary firm to hold the physical metal owned by the retirement account. Since owning rare coins in an IRA is prohibited because they are considered a collectible under the IRS rules, self-directed retirement plan investors commonly buy the bullion in the form of coins minted by various governments including the U.S. Mint.

Mortgages + Promissory Notes

Many self-directed investors prefer to loan funds from their accounts and collect interest payments from mortgages or promissory notes secured by hard assets like real estate or other tangible collateral. Although it's not required the loan be backed by any type of collateral, the majority of experienced lenders require the borrower to pledge some type of security in case of a default. Over time, most retirement plan lenders grow to favor making loans that are backed by collateral they understand. Some have a preference to loaning capital to business owners who pledge their company receivables in exchange for short-term operating capital. Other lenders prefer to place a lien on real estate, equipment or even publicly-traded stock to secure the loan they provide to a borrower.

Oil + Gas Investments

If you have experience in the energy industry, the oil and gas industry may provide you with opportunities to invest in what you know. Although the tax benefits available to those engaged in exploration and development of oil and gas fields provide an attractive way to shelter the income generated from these high-risk investments, many self-directed retirement plan investors prefer to buy mineral rights on potentially productive land. Others, with industry experience, prefer to buy equipment used in drilling or production that can be leased to companies in the petroleum industry. The vast majority of successful investors tend to focus on working with smaller, independent drillers close to home who need expansion capital as opposed to using their retirement funds to buy a percentage of ownership in a new well yet to be drilled.

The disadvantages are all tied to the market price of oil + gas, as well as the possible changes in future environmental regulations.

Alternative Energy: Just like you'll find in the oil and gas industry, self-directed retirement plan investors with an interest or experience in alternative energy seem to have the most success working with smaller companies with smaller capital requirements. In the wind energy industry, many operators realize their highest return on capital comes from producing power as opposed to owning the land where they have constructed windmills. This opens the door to investors with industry knowledge to purchase tracts of land that are later developed into wind farms.

Land owners are typically paid an annual lease fee by the energy company in exchange for the rights to someday construct a windmill on the property. Often, a substantially higher lease payment is made after a windmill is constructed on the property. Another option is to purchase land already being used by wind farm operators and lease it back to them, enabling them to expand into other areas.

The same type of opportunities exist in the solar energy industry, however, the purchase of equipment in either alternative energy industry is often better done outside the retirement plan because of state and federal tax credits now available.

Disadvantages here are very much like those described above for the oil + gas industry.

Venture Capital-Private Stock

In today's economy there are many opportunities to invest a portion of your retirement plan into start-up companies or established businesses that need growth capital. Because of the banking crisis that started in 2008, smaller companies have experienced extreme difficulty getting access to funding, unless they can present a very proven business model to the capital markets.

The angel investor networks that consist of successful entrepreneurs flush with cash from selling their companies have scaled back on the number of deals they are willing to fund. The demand for funding has increased as entrepreneurs continue to create new products and services, not only in the technology, health care and energy fields but in many industries that need to innovate to succeed in the new global economy.

This opens the door to retirement plan investors who often have a personal connection with the entrepreneur or business owner in need of funding. Since the funds held in a retirement plan are typically allocated for your long-term financial needs, there is often a perfect fit when invested into longer-term venture capital type projects. Regardless of how long it may take to see a huge return on this type of investment, you'll be most pleased when you don't have to pay taxes on the profits that occur since the gains are all paid into your retirement plan. Again, there are plenty of books and other resources available that can guide you through the due-diligence phase of selecting investments that fall into the venture capital category.

To create a deal flow and have frequent opportunities to review potential investments, network with those in the industry with which you have the most experience. Often your local CPA or securities attorney will have connections to entrepreneurs in your area who are seeking growth capital.

I recently learned of one investor who through a friend became aware of a sports drink company that needed capital to grow from a smaller regionally-focused company into one with a national focus. He invested a portion of his self-directed IRA funds into a private offering of the company's stock. The new capital was invested into getting sports celebrity endorsements and launching a national advertising campaign. Two years later, the company is now on track for a public offering of its stock that will return in excess of $1.2 million on each $50,000 investment. All of the gains flow back into this investor's IRA, Tax free.

Most of the success stories I've learned of that are in this category of investment are those where "local entrepreneur finds funding from local investors," and everyone wins when the company is sold or commences public trading of its stock.

Here is a quick example. Beverly spent most of her career as a wholesale furniture sales representative for a few large furniture manufacturing companies. I would put Beverly in the semi-pro category of self-directed investors. An interior designer at an architectural firm in a nearby city, Jill, became one of Beverly's customers. When Jill decided to open her own design studio, she shared her plans with Beverly, not with the intent to seek investment as much as to let her know she'd be leaving the architectural firm. Since Beverly had a self-directed IRA that was being used to own rental properties, she offered to invest a portion of her retirement funds into Jill's new business. The two agreed to structure their investment as a loan with a fixed 7% interest rate. In addition Beverly would receive 25% of the annual profits until the loan is fully repaid. They are now into the third year of their venture, and Beverly has averaged an 11% annual yield on her investment.

Franchise Investments

This asset class is really no different than the venture capital investing category except that the entrepreneur hasn't necessarily invested in a new product or service but instead has bought the franchise rights for a specific territory and agreed to follow the successful formula established by a franchisor.

For many retirement plan investors, this is a very attractive investment option, especially if the franchise has a successful operating history and is simply seeking funding for another location or territory. Retirement plan investors have stepped up to fill the void created when local banks cut back or stopped funding small business owners regardless of how successful they may be. Investments in this category vary. You may find entrepreneurs who will simply want to borrow funds from your retirement plan for expansion or they may offer to sell you shares in single or multiple locations. Other franchise owners and their investors may be most comfortable selling your retirement plan some of the real estate tied to their growing business. Be sure to have a good business attorney review all of the investment agreements before you invest your retirement plan into any of the venture capital opportunities you may find of interest.

Private Partnerships

There is a growing number of retirement plan investors who use investment into private partnerships as a way to diversify their funds across several asset classes. These investors are still practicing the "invest in what you know" method however, they are placing their funds into opportunities along with several other investors all seeking the common goal of higher returns, without the management responsibility. The total funds needed in a project are often far greater than what most individual investors can afford to commit so they join forces with a management team and other investors to finance the venture. Although partnerships exist in any industry, the real estate partnership is most common.

The partnership manager's experience and track record is an important aspect not to be overlooked. A client shared an interesting story with me that helps make this point. A group of six physicians in Texas saw the need for a medical office building near the hospital they all used in their practice. They each invested a portion of their retirement plan funds into a partnership that purchased six acres of land. Rather than hire an experienced developer/builder, they decided to save on fees by managing the project themselves. This decision led to a series of arguments when the project fell behind schedule and the budget spun out of control. In the end, they all became involved in litigation that resulted in a complete loss of their investments.

Partnerships can often be good investments for the retirement plan when managed by an experienced team paid an incentive in the form of profit participation. Typically, the large public partnerships promoted by brokerage firms are so burdened with fees paid to the marketing firms that the yields are only slightly high than that of a corporate bond fund.

All retirement plan custodians require a copy of the partnership agreement or private offering memorandum before they will honor your request to make an investment of your funds into a partnership. Although custodians review these documents, they do not in any way look to determine if the investment will be viable, so complete your own review of how the partnership funds are being spent and how the management team is compensated before you commit to an investment.

The Exotic Investment

Exotic investments are a result of retirement plan owners getting very creative while working within the IRS rules. Someday I'll put together a list of the top 50 exotic IRA investments; you'll be surprised at how far people have taken the "invest in what you know" concept. If it's your desire to structure an investment that generates high returns and allows you to have the level of control that makes you comfortable, I encourage you to again review the prohibited transaction rules found in Chapter 16.2.

Keep in mind that you as the account owner are always prohibited from receiving any type of benefit over and above the financial benefits that may be gained from the investments you make. Always discuss the potential prohibited transactions that can occur with your custodian before you purchase an asset.

Here's an example that I've heard mentioned at various retirement plan conferences for many years. A high school music teacher in Arizona was also in charge of managing the school's marching band. Many of the students rented the musical instruments they were being taught to play. The music teacher saw an opportunity to invest his self-directed IRA into musical instruments that he could then rent to his students each year.

The rental income, typically paid by the students' parents, all flowed into the teacher's IRA tax free each year. After a few years, the teacher had recovered the entire cost of his initial investment into instruments and continued to earn very good returns. Each year, several students purchased the instruments as they wanted to continue playing after graduation. This resulted in a constant return of his invested capital as well as a profit on each instrument sale.

There are many other out-of-the-ordinary investments that self-directed retirement plan owners have created. Don't be afraid to think creatively when it comes to placing your funds into an asset class with which you have experience. There is a good chance you'll find a way for your self-directed IRA to earn higher returns while reducing your risks.

Chapter 8.0

WHAT TYPES OF REAL ESTATE CAN I OWN IN MY RETIREMENT PLAN?

Basically, the IRS rules allow you to own any type of property you can imagine. And the property can be located anywhere in the world.

Before you make an offer to purchase any type of real estate with retirement plan funds, review the prohibited transaction rules. You'll find more details on these rules in Chapter 16.2, but for now know that:

- You cannot *use* the property owned by your retirement plan. For example: you cannot use the property as a vacation home or even as a pasture for the family horses.
- You cannot buy property from a related party. See Chapter 16.3 for the definition of related parties.
- None of the income or profits generated by the property can be paid to you as the account owner. <u>All income is deposited into the retirement plan that owns the property.</u>

Since there are so many great books and courses on real estate investing, we need not cover everything you should know before making a real estate investment decision. John T. Reed is one of my favorite real estate investing authors; others are listed in the **Resource section** of this book.

Below is a brief description of the advantages and disadvantages to each type of investment real estate:

Single-family Homes: These are the most popular real estate assets held in retirement plans. Most tenants dream of having a yard and the privacy of renting their own house as opposed to renting an apartment.

When the investor decides to sell a single-family property, there are typically far more potential buyers than compared to the multi-family type property. The disadvantages are all related to the responsibility of being a landlord. A prolonged vacancy period can destroy the annual returns that may have been projected at the time of purchase. In addition, the banks that provide financing on these properties to investors will often limit you to the number of properties they will finance for you.

Multi-family Homes: Some investors feel this type of property is easier to manage since the monthly rents are typically lower and, if the property has a large number of rental units, it may be possible to get an onsite manager to help run the day-to-day operations of the property. When a vacancy occurs in a multi-family property, you see a *partial* decline in monthly revenue as opposed to a 100% drop in income as you would a single-family unit, until a new tenant is moved in. The disadvantage may be that when it is time to sell, there is a limited number of potential buyers. Also, lenders that like multi-family properties commonly base their available loan amounts on the actual profits being earned by the property.

Of course the task of getting a loan to purchase a fully occupied property is easier than one that needs repairs and is only partially occupied even though the neglected property is a better long-term value.

Commercial Properties: The tenants in this type of property are, of course, business owners who need some type of local presence in the market so they can transact with their customers. A property with high traffic counts or the type of zoning that permits certain business operations can be highly desirable to certain types of businesses. The tenants in a commercial property are often required by contract to pay their portion of the common area maintenance costs including utilities, property insurance, taxes and periodic maintenance to the building. In many states, the eviction process can be completed quickly since tenants have fewer rights to remain in the building if they are in default of the lease agreement, compared to those tenants in single-family and multi-family homes.

The disadvantage is that many businesses fail each year and are unable to pay the rents they agree to. Management of the property can become expensive when there is a high rate of turnover, because commercial real estate agents who helped lease space in the building are typically paid their commissions from the initial rents paid by the tenants.

Development Land: Development land is often a good investment in the retirement plan in that it is typically a longer-term investment that matches the long-term nature of retirement plan savings goals. When you can purchase land and then change the zoning to permit a higher and better use of the property, the property's new value can be substantially higher than the original purchase price.

If you are patient and purchase property in the path of progress, the zoning changes may be initiated by neighboring property owners or by the county zoning department. *It is very important that you understand the current zoning restrictions before you make a land purchase.* Most county zoning departments maintain a zoning map that will forecast how they see the future zoning of the area occurring. Also, if you lack direct experience in this area, it is wise to partner with experienced people who know the zoning rules and have a track record of successfully changing zoning before you buy development land.

The disadvantage of investing in development land is the amount of time and capital that is often required to bring a property to completion so that it can be sold. When re-zoning of a property is initiated, neighboring property owners are notified and often object to any proposed changes. Environmental impact studies are often required by the county before a final re-zoning is approved. Financing for most land development projects is difficult to obtain until all the required entitlements are in place. Most importantly, you want as much assurance as possible that the market demand you see at the time of purchase will still be there when the project is completed.

Agricultural Land: Food and commodity prices are constantly rising in the current economic cycle. A growing number of retirement plan investors who have some experience in the agriculture industry are acquiring land that derives its value primarily from crops that can be produced at profitable levels. Even with the increase in agricultural land prices over the last few years, there are many smaller farmers interested in selling their property and immediately leasing back the property on a long-term basis.

These arrangements can be classic win/win deals for both parties. The farmer gets to free up capital that has been locked up in land their family may have owned for generations, while the retirement plan investor doesn't have to search for a long-term tenant to lease the property. The investor now receives any property appreciation that occurs in the future, along with immediate income paid by the farmer, and the farmer continues to generate income from the crops he grows.

An alternative enhancement to the above structure occurs when the farmer/seller is willing to provide financing for a portion of the total purchase price by accepting a promissory note as well as cash from the retirement plan investor. In this scenario, the farmer once again leases the property back from the investor and pays a fixed annual rent to use the property each year. The retirement plan now pays a fixed mortgage payment to the farmer/seller out of the rental income received each year. The benefit to this structure is that the retirement plan, because of the leverage it has obtained, can buy three to four times the amount of property because of the financing available vs. completing an all-cash purchase.

The disadvantage to agricultural land is the volatility in commodity prices. If the market price of corn, for example, drops drastically, the farmer won't realize a profit from his crop and may eventually default on the agreement to lease land from the retirement plan. In addition, buying productive farm land at a good price is a very competitive endeavor as the agricultural industry has become heavily dominated by large corporate farmers. Be sure to seek advice from experts in agricultural land before making investments in this asset class.

International Real Estate: Fantastic bargains can be found by those who look outside the United States for investment real estate. Because of several factors, including lower labor costs, less competition and an abundance of property in prime locations, retirement plan investors have been buying more foreign real estate in the last several years. For many investors who believe the value of the U.S. Dollar will continue to decline, this is an investment that makes sense since they are now using the currency of the country the property is located in to make a purchase transaction.

The disadvantage for many is that the IRS rules prohibit you, as the account owner, from using the property in any way. Don't think you can use the property as a possible vacation home, just because it's outside of the USA. In addition, you'll need to engage a real estate expert in the country you select for investment. Although many of the top rated custodians have experience with international real estate, it's imperative you check with your custodian before beginning a transaction. I've helped clients with transactions in South and Central America, where all of the contracts are in Spanish and require translation by the custodian. Always budget extra time to purchase international real estate.

Vacation homes: Owning a property in a resort community that has a high demand for short-term rentals has become a favorite investment vehicle for retirement plan investors. Those that I've seen reach the highest levels of consistent profit are real estate investors with existing experience in vacation rental properties. Chapter 10 covers this topic in much greater detail. Keep in mind that you as the account owner are not permitted to use the property while it's an asset in your retirement plan.

I'm often asked, "Who is going to know if I use the home for a week?" The IRS may never know, however, the penalties are severe for those who are caught breaking the rules. The value of the property at the time you've broken the rules is considered a *distribution* from your retirement plan. Depending on your age, you may be hit with an early-withdrawal penalty in addition to the taxes that are due. There are too many good opportunities in today's real estate market to consider doing anything that violates the rules. If your plan is to someday withdraw a property from the retirement plan and use it full or even part time, then consider the fractional ownership approach described in Chapter 11.

Real Estate Options: Real estate options allow a small amount of money (the option fee) to control a specific property for a fixed period of time. This is definitely an advanced real estate investing method, and although it's relatively simple, few real estate agents in my experience have ever seen this used. You'll want to read some of the books on this method or work with an experienced coach before making offers with your retirement plan funds.

Typically, the investor finds a bargain property and pays the seller a non-refundable option payment from the IRA and in return is granted the right to purchase the property at the agreed-upon price for a set period of time. Before the time runs out and the option period expires, the investor has the chance to find a buyer for the property at a price higher than he has agreed to pay, therefore keeping the difference as profit.

The disadvantage, of course, is that the option can expire before another buyer is found, and the option fee is lost. Because of this, most option fees paid by experienced investors are small amounts, representing less than five percent of the property's current market value. Since options have the potential for very high profits that would otherwise be taxed as short-term capital gains, investors with experience in this area will often use their self-directed IRA as a tax-free vehicle to hold the option and receive the profits.

Lease Options: Sometimes known as "sandwich leases," lease options are another one of the more advanced real estate investing methods that can be used with your IRA and for very little money, when compared to the cost of making an outright property purchase.

Peter Fortunato of St.Petersburg, Florida, (www.peterfortunato.com) is one of the best teachers of these creative real estate investing methods. Basically, your IRA leases a property at a fixed monthly cost and then leases the property to an occupant willing to pay a higher monthly rate. The difference between the rent collected and the rent paid is tax-free profit for your retirement plan. The IRA owner can often combine a lease purchase option with the sandwich lease for additional gains, if the property is sold to the tenant who occupies the property.

The clear disadvantage of this method is that the IRA is committed to renting the property for the period of time specified on the lease, and if it is unable to locate a tenant or experiences periods of vacancy, the IRA account balance gradually declines without income from a tenant. Also, the lease agreement between the property owner and the IRA account must clearly permit the sub-leasing of the property.

Marina-boat Slips: I always like to share this opportunity with friends who enjoy boating. If you have experience in the marina business, these types of real estate investments can be profitable, based upon a number of factors, including: location, market demand for boat slips and the length of the boating season in the area. Your self-directed IRA can purchase one or more boat slips and then rent that space for monthly income. I know of a few transactions where the retirement plan purchased the entire boat dock system and hired the marina operator to manage all of the rental and maintenance activity, with the profits flowing back to the retirement account.

The disadvantages of this type of investment are tied to the overall economy and to boat storage demand, weather conditions and the liability that results from mixing slippery wood surfaces with too much alcohol.

Now, I wonder who will be the first investor to buy and rent fishing huts across Minnesota lakes all winter in a self-directed IRA?

SECTION 4

Leveraging Your New Knowledge

Chapter 9

THE SMALL DIFFERENCES IN IRA REAL ESTATE INVESTING VS. TRADITIONAL REAL ESTATE INVESTING

For the vast majority of real estate investors, their first IRA owned property comes late in their real estate investment career. What motivates them to begin using an IRA is typically a property sale that generates a big tax bill, and they feel the pain of losing a substantial amount of money that they worked hard to create while owning the property.

Those who get the sinking feeling they'll owe big taxes from a property sale often seek advice from their tax professional. This is where they learn about doing a 1031 Exchange. Doing a 1031 exchange is fine until you want to begin living off the savings you've accumulated from your real estate investing activity. Far too often, when you stop the exchanging cycle, the taxes that come due can be huge.

That's why professionals in the exchange industry will often say, "Exchange 'til you die." Once you get into the exchange cycle as a real estate investor, it's very hard to break free while you're alive.

There are many real estate investors who have worked very hard over their investing career to build a large net worth by owning properties. They carefully studied the market, they made great deals when they purchased each property and they managed the property well, keeping their expenses well under control. Their annual income grew, and they took advantage of the available tax benefits to keep a large portion of their annual profits. They did everything right. Each time they sold a property they delayed the taxes due by purchasing another property of equal or greater value, as the Exchange rules require. At some point, however, they just grew too old or too tired to continue managing their properties.

At this point, many real estate investors are eager to cash in their chips and enjoy retirement. When they seek advice from their tax professional, they hear the bad news. They leave rather stunned after hearing that if they sell they will pay the majority of the sale proceeds in taxes, since they must recapture *all* of the tax benefits on *all* of the gains they've worked so hard to accumulate. Typically, they are told, "Just leave these properties to your children" because if they sell, the taxes are far too great.

Of course, the purpose of this book is not to teach you everything you should know about the 1031 exchange rules; however, it's important to know why investors are often told to leave properties to their children. When someone inherits your investment real estate assets, the properties are appraised at the time of your death, and those fortunate enough to receive the property are taxed only on any gains they receive over and above the value that is established at the time of your death. This event is known as a "step up in basis" and your tax advisor can explain all the details.

Investors who instead use their IRA or 401k plan to hold their investment real estate effectively eliminate four problems always faced by the investor caught up in the exchange cycle.

- When you sell a property held in the IRA, you are not required to invest into another property within 180 days as you are required to do when using the 1031 exchange rules.
- If you are selling a property because you feel the market has peaked, The 1031 exchange rules force you to buy a replacement property, within a short period of time, even though the replacement property can be in an entirely different market area.
- When you sell a property held in the IRA, you are not required to purchase a replacement property at the same or greater value as the property you are selling, as is the case with the 1031 rules.
- When you sell a property held in the IRA, you are not required to recapture the tax benefits taken during your ownership, as you would if you sold and decided not to enter into a 1031 exchange.
- Obviously, for investors who choose to ignore the 1031 exchange rules as well as not use their retirement plans to hold

their investment real estate, they face paying federal taxes on their profits as well as potential state and local taxes.

I'll often get a strong argument from seasoned real estate investors when we discuss the benefits of using a retirement plan to hold their rental property investments. They often point out that one of the major benefits of owning investment real estate is getting that tax benefits each year. I have to agree that getting monthly income that's sheltered from taxes because of the various depreciation and operating expense deductions is nice; however, when the day comes to sell that property, all of the depreciation expenses must be recaptured and reported as income in the year the property is sold.

In my experience, it is far easier and more profitable long-term to hold the real estate in a self-directed IRA or 401(k) plan. You don't get to write off all the expenses and depreciation when you own the property in the IRA, but none of the annual income or profits from the sale of the property are taxed since they all flow back into the retirement plan. Sure, there is tax due when you take a distribution from all retirement plans (except the Roth IRA); however, your wealth grows much faster, and you can have access to the savings while you are alive.

I want to share a story about two of my favorite clients, Carlton and Maggie, who live in Southern California. Carlton is now 90 and Maggie will soon turn 87. Although we've invested together many times over the last 25 years, neither of them has an IRA; their 9-to-5 careers were winding down when the IRA was created in 1974. They have always been active real estate investors. As an engineer, Carlton found it easy to build single-family homes and repair rental properties after work each day. Maggie worked in advertising during the day and learned property management on her own, before anyone offered the type of classes taught today.

Each time they sold a house, they'd complete an exchange in order to delay the tax bill. By the time they'd reached their 60's, they owned over $12M of investment real estate. The single-family homes were eventually exchanged for small apartment buildings. Those were exchanged into larger garden apartment complexes and small shopping centers over time. They managed these properties without the help of a professional manager because they felt every dollar they paid a manager was less they could leave to their two adult children.

When they reached their 80's, the work was just too much. I can't recall them ever taking a vacation, because of their property management responsibilities. One day, Maggie called in tears because they had just left their CPA's office. They had agreed to sell one of the apartment buildings for $4M. Their accountant estimated the taxes due would total $3.7M, since they had done so many exchanges on prior property sales. None of that $3.7M would go to their family or their church. It was lost forever in taxes.

This, more than any other personal experience I'd had with 1031 exchanges, taught me the danger of exchanging investment properties rather than holding them in the self-directed retirement plan.

I'm not opposed to using the 1031 exchange option in certain cases. Just plan ahead and understand the consequences to doing an exchange. At the end of the day, a combination of real estate investments, both inside the IRA as well as outside the IRA, will often give you the best of both worlds and a more predictable retirement portfolio.

Chapter 10

HOW TO OWN VACATION RENTAL PROPERTIES IN THE IRA

Many dream of owning a beachfront property or a cabin at our favorite ski resort in an IRA and using the property as a vacation home. This has become a very popular idea in this current era of depressed real estate prices in many resort areas.

You *can* own vacation property in your IRA; however, you can't *use* the property while it's owned by the IRA. Later we'll show you how you can have your cake and eat it, too. (The secret is in taking ownership in the form of "fractional deeds.") But first, we should cover the basics on owning vacation rental properties.

Vacation rental property can be a great investment if you make a plan in advance and fully execute on the plan. Aside from getting a good deal in a beautiful location, it's all about management of the property. There is a lot more involved in managing vacation rentals vs. local long-term rentals. First and foremost, it's very important to find a property manager who specializes in vacation properties. (see Chapter 15 on property managers.) You'll want to make sure you're not competing against a manager who has their own rentals in the same building or local area.

The most common horror story I've heard when it comes to vacation rentals, has to do with owners hiring managers who fill their own properties with guests before filling their clients' rentals with guests. This can be common when you own a vacation rental in a large project with on-site management services; you may often be *required* to use those services if you rent the unit on a short-term vacation basis.

It's just basic supply and demand economics. If you own 1 of 50 basically identical condos in a building, you are competing with every other owner for guests. Some owners, in desperate situations, may rent for far less than you have estimated, just to bring in revenue to pay their property taxes. Regardless of whether your vacation home is on the beach or on the ski slopes, my advice is to always own something unique where the competition is limited vs. a vacation rental in a large resort complex.

The good news is that the Internet has made it much easier to own and profit from vacation rentals. Websites like www.VRBO.com (and there are many others) make it much easier for you or your property manager to attract vacation renters. Even if you don't use these sites to attract renters and manage the bookings of your property, be sure to use them in your research to learn about your competition. Availability calendars that represent homes available on a vacation basis will show you how often the competition has bookings vs. vacancies, as well as seasonal rates during both the high and low season for that area.

These sites can be a great tool for the vacation homeowner. Not only do they fill your calendar with renters but also collect your rents and deposits, while tracking your guests' comments about the service they have received.

Keep in mind that you may be expected to provide maid and maintenance services, as well as someone to handle the check-in and check-out service, so be sure to add these expenses to your budget before making an offer to purchase the property.

Chapter 10.1

VACATION RENTAL PROPERTY SUCCESS STORIES

Let's look at how profitable it can be to own vacation rental properties in your retirement plan. Joe lives in Kansas City but loves the Florida lifestyle, which is also where he decided to start buying vacation homes for a nice secondary income. His first three rental homes were purchased outside of his IRA. Today I'd rank Joe as a Pro self-directed IRA investor when compared to many others I know. He made good returns and developed a good system to manage the vacation clients he catered to however, his income taxes increased right along with his monthly income. Then he discovered that his IRA could actually own his next investment properties in Florida, and that all the income would be free of any taxes until he retired and began to live off the retirement plan.

Joe now purchases all of his rental properties in his IRA. Since he owns several condo units in a single building, he can offer weekly lodging to larger group of vacationers, since they often want to stay in the same building. To keep his property fully rented, Joe advertises his vacation condos on a few of the popular vacation home websites and gets referrals from local real estate agents and property managers. All of the rental income goes to a credit card merchant account, and each month he transfers profits into the IRA. Joe tells me he keeps a small reserve in the account to pay his operating costs, while he saves capital to buy his next rental property.

Joe has developed a series of emails that go to renters before, during and after their rental period. The initial message is a confirmation of their reservation along with a list of things to do in the local area, if it's the guest's first stay in his property. A few days before check-in, an email provides helpful information about the condo, contact numbers for the property manager and details about check-in. During the guest's stay, Joe checks in again via email or text to make sure everything is to the guest's satisfaction and encourages posting of comments on the Facebook page for the property.

After check-out, Joe's email confirms the deposit has been returned to the guest's credit card and again encourages his guest to share photos of the vacation or the condo with friends and family on Facebook. Encouraging guests to share their vacation experience with friends and family builds repeat business for Joe. He's been very successful at getting feedback (testimonials) from his guests on how much they enjoyed the place.

And, of course, the testimonials all find their way onto Joe's website that new potential guests see before they book their Florida vacation.

In order to streamline the management of his properties, Joe has hired maids who communicate via email and text on the status of each unit being cleaned, as well as when each unit is ready for guests. He has also contracted with a local maintenance crew for any repairs that may be needed, either while guests are at the property or during any vacancy periods. A local person checks the guests in and out, while all funds (rents and deposits) are done via credit card on Joe's website.

Now all of this may sound like a lot of work, but because of the system Joe has put in place, the property management task is minimized to a just a few hours a week. You may be asking yourself, "Why not just let the property manager do all of the work and watch the cash roll in?" I asked Joe that very question. He explained that being somewhat hands-on, even though he is a thousand miles away, allows him to maintain much higher occupancy rates which leads to good consistent profits.

If there is any secret formula to what Joe has developed, it's the referral program he has put in place that encourages his guests to tell their friends about his condos whenever they are booking a vacation in Florida. Guests who refer friends who book stays at Joe's properties get free nights when they return to stay in any of Joe's properties.

Another important element of Joe's system is the record he keeps of all the guests who have stayed in his condos. When he puts a property up for sale someday, he'll offer it to past guests, who may be in the market to buy a home where they have vacationed. He estimates he'll sell these properties some day without thee expense of a Realtor since he'll have a list of customers who are vary familiar with the benefits of the property.

How does Joe "get around" the rules that prohibit him from using one of his condos when he takes his Florida vacation? He has a unit in the building held outside of his IRA in which he and his family stay.

What can we learn from Joe's success? If your plan is to own vacation property far from home, it's best to take inventory of how much time you can commit to the management and the availability of local experts to do the rest. Joe's background is in sales and marketing so his skills in that area have been easily applied to keeping his property rented when neighboring condos sit vacant. You may have very different skills, and you'd be better off to hire others to market your property to potential guests.

How about a nice Hawaiian Punch

To help you understand the potential pitfalls of own a vacation home in your retirement plan let me tell you about Gary and the mess he created by ignoring some of the basic rules on owning vacation properties.

Gary and his family would love taking their annual vacations to Hawaii each year. His daughter eventually moved to Maui and started a family with her new husband. Gary saw an opportunity to purchase vacation condos and create a property management business for his daughter and son-in-law. Because he didn't research the rules that prohibit Gary's IRA from transacting business with a family member (his daughter) he hired her to manage his collection of rental properties and earn income from her management tasks, which is clearly a prohibited transaction.

To make matters even worse Gary owned a wholesale electrical supply business and he liked to reward his best customers by giving them a free week stay in one of his condos in exchange for the business they did with him each year. This of course was another prohibited transaction. Gary was personally receiving a benefit over and above a purely financial benefit to his IRA account. He often allowed his employees to stay in the condos at no cost.

I doubt that any of these prohibited transactions were intentional however, the IRS would see these activities as a violation of the rules and treat the value of the property as a distribution from Gary's IRA and require that he pay tax and possible penalties when they discover what he has done.

When we last spoke Gary was soon to meet with his IRA custodian and tax attorney to resolve these issues. He could correct these mistakes by:

1) Not paying his daughters property management company for their services or simply hire a non-related party to be his property management firm

2) He could pay his employees a bonus and let them rent any vacation property they desire

3) Find a way to reward his best customers without providing the free stay in his Hawaii condos

Don't think that you can get away with using a vacation property owned by your IRA and not get caught. So often I'm asked, "How is anyone (the IRS) going to know I've spent a week at the property?" Well, they may not but in an audit it's surprising what dots can be connected and you'll be in a position of having to explain how you spent a week in the same town where your IRA owns a vacation property and you won't be able to produce a hotel bill or the name of a friend you stayed with. If you properly own vacation properties in the IRA you'll be spending your own vacations at the Four Seasons resort while your IRA continues to grow from the tax advantaged profits you earn each year. See chapter 16.2 on prohibited transactions.

Chapter 11

WITHDRAWING IRA OWNED REAL ESTATE FROM YOUR RETIREMENT PLAN

In most cases any distribution you take from your IRA will trigger a taxable event since the value you are then receiving has never been taxed in the past.

The taxes due will depend on whether your IRA is a Traditional IRA or a Roth IRA, as well as your age at the time of withdrawal. You can take any of the real estate held in your IRA as a distribution instead of cash.

Regardless of the type of asset you withdrawal from an account, the same rules apply with regard to taxes. So, every time you take a distribution from the account, the value, whether it's cash, real estate, gold or anything else, is always reported by your custodian to the IRS. All withdrawals from your IRA are required to be reported on you tax return for the year the withdrawal has occurred.

If you skipped prior chapters and jumped ahead to this section remember, the rules prohibit you from using any type of property or asset even for a single day while the property is an asset of your IRA account.

Many account owners plan to eventually use property held in an IRA as a vacation home, a second home or even their primary residence. If you do plan to someday use the real estate then it's very important to map out a plan in advance so that you reach your goals, while paying the least amount of tax.

Ask yourself these questions before you purchase a property you may someday use:

- How much time during the year will I use the home? Might

- this property become my primary residence or just a home I will use occasionally as a vacation home?
- Will I be renting the home for income during the times I am not using it?
- What will be the estimated annual rental income and expenses generated by the property?
- Will the purchase be made with all cash or will I need or want to use a mortgage when buying the property?
- Will my IRA be the sole owner or will I also be using a spouse's IRA to make the purchase?
- Approximately how many years will the IRA own the home before I plan to withdrawal the property from the account?
- What do I estimate the value of the property will be when it is withdrawn from the account?
- Would taking ownership in the form of fractional deeds (see Chapter 11) be a smart option? Does state law permit ownership in a fractional deed manner?
- If I use a fractional deed structure, how many deeds should be issued, a total of 12 (1 per month) or 4 (1 per quarter)?

It may sound a bit complicated to own a vacation home in the IRA; when you review the above questions, however, it is relatively simple. Map out your plan in writing and present it to your tax professional.

Far too often, I'll speak with people who have been told by their CPA, "The rules don't allow you to own a vacation home in your IRA" or, "I've never heard of this, so it's not a smart investment; let's not trigger an audit."

Let me tell you about Bill and Sherry, a couple from Connecticut, who love Florida in the winter months. They are in the semi-pro classification of self-directed IRA investors. For years they took their family to the Gulf Coast each winter and stayed at a resort condo in Sarasota. Since they were both in their early forties, and could see themselves spending the entire winter in Sarasota after they retired, so they bought a condo on the beach in a resort community. Knowing that they would never spend the entire year in Florida, even after they were both retired, they estimated they would use the home for four to five months per year. Between their two IRA accounts, they had enough to buy the condo without using a mortgage.

When it came time to close escrow on the property, they instructed the title company to issue 12 separate deeds (one per month) so that they could, in the future, begin to withdrawal the fractionalized ownership "shares" from their retirement plans, a little at a time to prevent all the taxes from coming due in a single year. This gave them a lot of flexibility and control over when the tax bill comes due. In some years, they may want to withdrawal two fractions and in other years they may not withdrawal any ownership at all.

Not only had Bill and Sherry done their homework on how to minimize their taxes but also on how to maximize their annual income from buying the condo. Before making their purchase, Bill and Sherry interviewed property managers who specialize in renting vacation condos; this move allowed them to estimate how much the annual profit might be after paying a manager and the typical maintenance fees. After factoring in vacancies and all other possible expenses, they estimated that in most years they would see $14,000 per year of profits deposited into their IRA accounts.

Keep in mind that as long as all of the ownership is in their IRAs, they will not be spending any of their winter vacations in the condo. Instead, they will rent a similar condo in the same building and visit their condo just to make an inspection and meet with their property manager.

After age 59 ½ Bill and Sherry can begin taking an annual distribution from their IRAs and paying taxes on the value of the condo ownership they have transferred from the IRA into their individual names. Since they estimate the total value of the condo will be approximately $360,000, in the year they retire, each 1/12 fractional deed will have a value of $30,000 when they transfer the title into their individual name and begin spending a month in their condo. They estimate their federal tax to be $7,000 each time they withdrawal a deed from the IRA. This is the same amount of tax they would owe on a $30,000 cash withdrawal each year.

Bill and Sherry's plans are to eventually withdraw as many as five deeds from their IRAs and continue to rent the condo for income in the remaining months. Of course, if they ever want to make the home their primary year-round residence, they can withdrawal all 12 of the deeds from the IRA.

If their retirement plans change and they no longer plan to use the condo, their IRAs can simply sell the property, and the title company can issue a single deed to the new buyer of the property.

For many real estate investors planning for a comfortable retirement income stream, the idea of owning several properties that generate a monthly income is very attractive. They, too, should explore the idea of using a fractionalized deed system when they purchase the property, especially if they expect the property to be in their account when they reach the age of 70. As we saw in Chapter 3, all retirement plans except for the Roth IRA, require a RMD (Required Minimum Distribution) in the year the account owner turns age 70 ½.

Don't paint yourself into a corner by failing to plan for these RMD events. If some of the properties held in your IRA are in the form of fractional deeds, at least you can withdraw just enough to the meet the minimum RMD rules.

Whether your IRA holds title to the property in a single deed or several ownership deeds, be prepared to have the property appraised each time you request a "non-cash" distribution from the account. Being able to properly document the value of any asset you withdraw from the IRA is worth far more than the small expense to get a third-party written valuation. Nearly all custodians and CPAs are going to recommend you have an appraisal on any property you receive from the account.

The cost shouldn't be very high for an appraisal each year on properties that are owned on a fractionalized basis, after the initial appraisal is completed. The appraiser will need to update the market analysis portion of the appraisal report with several comparable property sales, since the physical size and location of the property will not change each year.

In summary, create a written plan before you purchase a vacation property in your IRA. Get answers to the questions above before you make a purchase offer. Know your IRA custodian's guidelines in advance, and if your CPA is skeptical, be prepared to educate him with the help of your custodian. It's easy to get caught up in the excitement of owning a vacation home in your retirement account; just make sure you've asked all the questions (and verified all the answers) before signing the property purchase contracts.

Chapter 12

INVESTING YOUR RETIREMENT PLAN IN REAL ESTATE

Stephen Covey, bestselling author of *The Seven Habits of Highly Successful People,* continually points out that to reach any goal you must start with the end in mind. This advice holds true when it comes to making investments. It's not good enough to say, "I want to have more income" or "I want a $1 million IRA when I retire." You need to be as specific as possible.

An example would be: "I want to average a 12% net return from a rental property each year over the next 5 years, while spending no more than 10 hours each month managing the property." Having this specific goal will keep you focused on buying only those properties that can help you meet this objective.

In the pursuit of any goal, everyone experiences roadblocks and obstacles. What separates the successful from the less-than-successful, the great from the mediocre, is the ability to get through, over or under these roadblocks and obstacles, no matter what. Make a commitment to yourself that you will do whatever is necessary to reach that goal.

One of the greatest rewards of my work comes from talking with clients within the first few days of buying their first property in their retirement plan. They all share the same feeling, 100% of the time, typically saying, "If I knew it was that easy to buy real estate in my IRA, I would have done this years ago!" You'll see in the next few chapters just how easy it is when you apply some simple steps we'll go over in detail.

Many experienced real estate investors are naturally hesitant the first time they use funds from a retirement plan to buy a property. If you were to list the steps they've taken in the past to buy a property and compare it to the steps in the upcoming chapter, you would see the addition of only two or three steps to the standard real estate purchase.

I like to point out to those with lots of real estate investing experience that the easy parts of the entire real estate investing experience are the use of the retirement plan and the custodian services. The difficult parts, including the purchase of the right property at the right price and the management tasks, are obviously still there and require far more time when compared to the steps that involve your retirement plan or custodian.

If you've skipped earlier parts of this book and turned directly to this how-to section, you may have missed some of the best advice I can give you. Before getting into the various steps required for success, I want you to know that it's important to **"invest in what you know."** This is the mantra for the majority of successful retirement plan investors with whom I've worked. As soon as they feel they have experience in owning and managing a certain type of asset class, they begin to make those same investments in their retirement plan.

Chapter 13

IRA REAL ESTATE PURCHASE CHECKLIST

Here are the steps for acquiring real estate in a self-directed IRA. The first few steps will not need to be repeated on your second or subsequent transactions since they relate to the initial opening and funding of the account.

- **Select a self-directed custodian and open the account.** Chapter 4.1 covers the most important steps in the custodian selection process.

- **Establish a general budget.** Set an amount based upon the approximate price of the real estate you wish to purchase. If you plan to finance a portion of the purchase amount, check with lenders on the required down payment guidelines.

- **Fund the self-directed account.** Most custodians include the cost of transferring your funds from an existing IRA or 401(k) in a small fee charged when opening the account. It is not necessary to transfer the full account balance in an existing account into the new account. You can always transfer additional funds or make annual contributions to the account later, if your budget requirements increase.

- **Confirm your custodian transaction guidelines.** Your custodian can give you an estimate of the time needed to fund your investment, depending on the type of transaction you expect to make. If your transaction is an all-cash purchase of a residential property located in the USA, the custodian shouldn't need more than seven to ten business days to complete the investment. Transactions that include mortgage financing or property outside the country may require twice as much time to complete. Give yourself plenty of time to close escrow, and all parties will be pleased with the end results.

- **Go shopping for property.** If you fail to take the above steps in order and instead begin making offers on property, you'll be putting yourself and others under unnecessary stress to complete a purchase transaction. This is by far the most common mistake first time retirement plan investors make. If purchase agreements have been signed and deposits paid to the seller or an escrow account, you'll be required to cancel the transaction if you are unable to fund the deal in a timely manner. You would have to start over after completing the first four steps above. Depending on what terms are stated in the purchase agreement, you could lose some or all of the deposit you've paid.

- **You make your offer to purchase.** When you have found the perfect property, the written offer designating your retirement plan as the buyer is made to the seller. Your custodian will sign the offer on behalf of your retirement plan and deliver a deposit check to either the seller's real estate agent or a third-party escrow agent to hold until the closing date. If acceptable terms cannot be reached with the seller of the property, the deposit and purchase offer agreement are returned to your custodian, while you begin to search for another property.

- **You have an accepted purchase offer.** Your custodian will schedule delivery of your funds to the escrow agent after any and all purchase contingencies are completed and you as account owner sign the required authorization to fund the purchase of the property. You will be responsible for arranging the various insurance coverages determined by you to be appropriate for the property. The insurance premiums will be paid from your retirement plan, along with any other closing costs you have authorized.

- **Close of Escrow.** The custodian will require the escrow agent to title the property in the name of your retirement plan and deliver recorded copies of the property deed to the custodian for deposit into your account.

- **Congratulations!** Your retirement plan now owns the property, and all profits are non-taxable since all income from ownership or sale of the property are deposited into your self-directed IRA or 401(k) account. Your custodian will provide you with copies of all the documents related to the property and your account.

While the last few steps in the above list are being completed, you'll need to begin implementing your plans to generate profits from the property. If your plan is to rent the property, it is your responsibility to oversee the task of making any needed repairs to the property and secure a tenant. If repairs *are* required, the payment for all material and labor will need to be paid from your retirement plan and not from your personal funds. Your custodian will require that all rental income and tenant security deposits be deposited into your self-directed IRA account.

In chapter 15 we cover information on using a property manager, which can make the payment of property expenses much easier, as opposed to having the custodian pay every monthly expense related to the property. In essence, the property manager collects the income from the tenant and then subtracts out all the monthly ownership expenses. The monthly income is then paid by the property manager directly to the custodian.

Chapter 14

BUILDING YOUR PERSONAL INVESTMENT TEAM

> Talent wins games, but teamwork and intelligence wins championships.
> ~Michael Jordan

I realize I've been a little harsh in my criticism of Wall Street and the financial services industry thus far, so let me explain where these feelings come from. Over the years, I've had so many investors tell me they wish they could go back in time and take a different approach to how they managed their portfolio.

They'd love to have their money back, now that they see the bottom-line results that can occur when they simply hand their savings to someone else to manage.

At the end of the day, each investor could have enjoyed much better results had they built a team of people around them that had a common goal. Your goal of course is to build wealth first by not losing your capital, and then by maximizing the return on your capital, with the least amount of risk and taxes.

This chapter is focused on how to build your personal Investment Team so you are not in the game along nor are you burdened with overseeing every task necessary to reach the results you are working to achieve.

Your best investment performance comes from:

- Making team building a top priority since this will increase your returns

- Having a quality coach or experienced advisors
- Recognizing a mistake and taking corrective action

Regardless of the type of assets you decide to own in your retirement plan, you can't be expected to do all the work. You'll have greater success in a shorter amount of time if you build a team of people you can consult for advice. Don't expect them all to agree on your course of action. You need to be the captain of your own ship by gathering advice and information from each person on the team and then making the final decisions on the course you'll take.

For example, too often many investors fail to get tax advice from their CPA when they decide to change course. In order to purse a new investment opportunity, they sell assets they already own, which may trigger a larger-than-necessary tax payment. Often the investor's CPA doesn't see what the investor has done until tax time rolls around and by then it's too late to plan the best course of action.

The type of team I'm suggesting you build is more than just you and your financial advisor, especially if you are going to own real estate or other tangible assets not offered by your advisor.

Members of your team may include:
- Real estate agent
- Retirement plan Custodian
- Insurance agent
- Title-Escrow agent
- Attorney
- CPA
- Property manager
- Lenders-Investors

If you are already an active real estate investor you are already working these people, although you may not have considered them teammates in your business. You are not out recruiting volunteers for your team, instead you are selecting the best team members you can afford to pay in return for their services.

I suggest you gather these people together occasionally for lunch or a dinner and talk about your goals and desire to work more closely together. Discuss your plans on using your self directed IRA to build wealth. Share what you have learned in this area. You may be very surprised how many members of your team will find this investing approach of interest. Don't be surprised if the number of new opportunities you get to choose from, also increases as a result of these team meetings every few months. Expect to be invited onto the teams that others build since you'll have the experience in using self directed retirement plans that few others can offer.

Chapter 15

SHOULD I HIRE A PROPERTY MANAGER?

In my experience, real estate investors fall into two basic groups; those who always like to self- manage their properties and those who use professional management services.

Your goal should be to hire others to do the management for you. It's hard to imagine rapidly building a sizeable retirement plan if you are also taking on the responsibility of managing each property in your portfolio, while also having time to do the more enjoyable things in life.

With that said, I know many investors who prefer to manage their own properties for some of the following reasons:

- They like the added relationships that come with being a landlord. You might say they just like to be active and being a landlord satisfies that need. They become friends with not only their tenants but also those maintaining the property. This very often helps to expand their business.

- They like the control that comes from doing the management themselves. Some are very proud of the property they own and enjoy maintaining it at the highest standards. They realize they are in the service business and simply like serving their customers.

- They can't afford a professional manager because they made a mistake when buying the property. In other words, they didn't do their homework before the purchase. These investors want to avoid losing even more money each month on a deal that has gone bad (where the income doesn't cover the expense).

If you buy the right property at the right price, there should be plenty of room for a manager's fee and a good profit after all expenses. Regardless of whether you hire a manager or do the work yourself, I recommend learning as much as you can about property management. There are many excellent property management books and courses on the market today, written by experienced professionals who share their best ideas. (See the Resource section for Property Management courses and books)

Much can be gained from a weekend course on property management, even if you have already planned on hiring a professional. Finding a good manager that you like before you make an offer to buy a property is always a plus. Good managers know which neighborhoods are attractive to prospective tenants as well as areas that should be avoided.

In chapter 15.2 you'll find a list of interview questions to ask a prospective manager. It's important to interview several property managers in your market to see how they compare with each other. Too often a rookie real estate investor will take the advice of the real estate agent that helped them purchase the property, when it's time to hire a manager. Of course people recommend others for many different reasons and it's very important to get the right manager on your team. You are putting a great deal of trust in the manager you select so consider this choice just as important as the property you select. I've witnessed bad managers ruin a good property and at the same time a good manager can bail you out of some of the rookie mistakes that can occur. Like many other services we buy each day, I think you'll find you get what you pay for.

Chapter 15.1

PROPERTY MANAGERS ARE A GREAT SOURCE OF GOOD DEALS

The property management business is like any other business: they like to keep their current clients and are always looking for new clients. A property manager often knows about a client's desire to sell, long before the owner contacts an agent to list the property for sale.

Several of the properties I've acquired were sent to me by property managers. Over time, they have come to understand what I want to achieve as well as the type of properties I'll buy. In exchange, the manager knows I'll ask them to continue to handle the management responsibilities.

Managers typically want to keep income they currently earn from a property so naturally want to continue in their management role. If that property is sold to an owner/occupant, the manager's role, of course, ends right along with the income they receive each month.

A good property manager is a very important member of the team you are building. If you are in the early stages of building your team or a novice at investing in rental property, get some assistance from the manager when completing the rental property analysis form. If the results of your analysis do not show the promise of returns you need to reach the investment goals you've set, this may not be the right property to purchase. But at least the property manager now knows you are a serious potential customer to be contacted whenever properties with high potential returns become available. Just keep shopping until the right opportunity comes along.

Be aware that some states enforce regulations that require all property managers to be licensed real estate agents or brokers. If this is so in the area in which you are investing, there may also be rules that prohibit them from making financial projections on a property you are considering purchasing. That's fine, since to become efficient at uncovering good deals, you'll want to have the experience necessary to analyze any property on your own. Typically real estate agents or a property manager can help you gather the necessary income and expense data even if they are prohibited from making a financial forecast about the property.

It's important, whenever possible, to speak with the *owner* of the property management firm you interview. Even smaller management companies often have a "front line" staff of service personnel taking calls from property owners looking for management help. Even though these employees can be very helpful, it's the owner of the company you are ultimately trusting with your property so get through the gatekeepers whenever possible. No one cares more about the success of that management company than the owner does, so build your relationship with the person at the top of the chain of command who can help you the most.

Chapter 15.2

INTERVIEW QUESTIONS FOR PROPERTY MANAGERS

The books and courses on using property management firms typically provide an extensive list of questions you'll want to ask during an interview. The questions listed below are some of the most important questions you'll want to have answered before you make a final decision on whom to trust with your property.

Many of these questions should be asked not only during the initial telephone interview but again when you meet the owner of the firm. In my experience, most investors who talk about unpleasant property management experiences eventually admit there was a failure to communicate in the early stages of the owner/manager relationship.

Over time, you'll develop your own list of favorite questions to ask in the interview. Here are mine:

Where do you advertise for new tenants?

How do most prospective tenants find your firm?

How do you screen tenants?

What steps are taken to avoid discrimination?

Do you hold the tenant security deposits or do I, as owner of the property?

What are the vacancy rates I should expect?

What repairs should be done before I rent the property?

Do you hire others or use your staff to complete most repairs?

How do you inform me of repairs?

What are your eviction procedures?

How do we communicate? Phone-email-text-USPS?

What do the monthly statements that I receive as the property owner look like?

How do you conduct background and reference checks on prospective tenants?

Is your firm a member of Better Business Bureau?

What attorney do you use for evictions?

How much does a typical eviction cost?

Have you been sued by past property owners or tenants?

Has the state or county charged your firm with any violations?

Do you as manager appear in court or do I as owner when evictions are required?

When would you expect to increase the rent for my property?

What do you charge for your services?

How many units like mine do you manage?

Of course, some of these questions are best asked after the prospective manager has visited the property you intend to purchase.

One of the most important questions from the list is, "How many units *like mine* do you manage?" You then want to ask, "How many of those do you or your partners or family members own?" It's unfortunate but true that there is a tendency among some property managers to first fill their own vacancies before filling those of their customers. You don't want to be in a position where the manager is willing to let your investment property sit empty, while their own properties are always fully rented.

Owning investment real estate is exactly like any other business. You can never know too much about how to maximize profits, reduce your risks and become more efficient in how you manage your time.

Chapter 16

IRS RULES FOR THE IRA

*The IRS! They're like the Mafia,
they can take anything they want!
~Jerry Seinfeld*

The IRS established rules for the operation of the IRA when these accounts were first created by Congress in 1974. Like so many of the IRS rules we have to adhere to, you can really begin to understand the reason for these rules when you understand the intent of the IRS which most often of course is to collect as much tax revenue as possible.

Since most capital in retirement plans has never been taxed by the IRS, these rules are in place to insure they eventually collect the taxes due. When overly creative IRA account owners concoct a scheme to cut the IRS out of the picture and not pay the taxes eventually due, there can be severe penalties applied by the IRS.

Many investors upon their initial review of the rules voice some frustration because their intended investment strategy would clearly be a disqualified transaction in the eyes of the IRS. Other come away from a review of the rules feeling they are just to complicated and are unwilling to take the time as you are doing to complete some basic research into all the options that are available. Too often in my experience the investor gives up on the entire self-directed concept and continues to hope they can build a sizeable retirement savings account with traditional Wall Street investments.

The reality is that the vast majority of Self-Directed IRA investors never come close to breaking the IRS rules. Credit has to be given to the IRA account owners Custodians or account Administrators who are responsible for reviewing each transaction in the account. As a general rule the more layers of creativity there are in the transaction you are engineering the closer you'll want to pay attention to the rules and seek competence advice for your Custodian or tax advisor.

Chapter 16.1

USE YOUR CUSTODIAN AS YOUR IRA TAX GUIDE

The most valuable service you'll receive from your Self-Directed Custodian is a review of the transaction documents before any investment is initiated by your retirement plan. Whenever I hear a client criticize their Custodian, it's often over the amount of time it takes for the transaction documents to be reviewed, which is seldom more than 2 business days.

The Custodian's we often recommend are very meticulous when it comes to a through review of each transaction you've requested they make with your account. The last thing any Custodian wants is an unhappy client or litigation brought on as result of a violation of the IRS rules.

Use your Custodian's expertise and ask for a review of the transaction you are about to make before signing documents, or making commitments with the seller of the asset you want to hold in your account. Custodians often rely on their won CPAs and Tax Attorneys when an unusual investment request comes in from an account holder. Don't be surprised if you Custodian declines to make an investment that they feel is in a grey area of the IRS rules. Use any investment denial as a learning experience. A good Custodian will show you where the rules prohibit the type of transaction you were initially contemplating and often make suggestions on how to restructure the transaction in order to reach the goal. Again, Custodians cannot give you investment advice however they can and will do their best to make sure the assets you wish to own meet all of the IRS requirements.

There is such a broad range of opportunities in today's marketplace for Self-Directed retirement accounts, that there is no reason to give up on managing your own investments simply because your initial investment plans were considered to be a potential prohibited transaction by your

Custodian. If the investment you plan to make with your Self-Directed retirement plan is a purely passive investment, there is a good chance it will be approved by your Custodian.

Chapter 16.2

PROHIBITED TRANSACTIONS

From working with thousands of investors exploring the use of a self-directed IRA to diversify retirement plans, I've witnessed a good amount of fear surrounding the area of prohibited transactions. Even though the penalties can be severe, it's the general rules related to prohibited transactions which may scare the average investor away from using a self-directed retirement plan.

Too often, the initial focus is put upon all the things the rules prohibit you from doing rather than all of the opportunities there are to invest in what you understand and can control. With that said, it is important to understand the rules so that as you shop for opportunities, you will know where the boundaries are, as well as how to avoid stepping out of bounds.

I often encounter real estate investors who have a long track record of success in various investing methods; however, they are now exploring the idea of making all of their profits in a tax-advantaged account. I like to make the point in our initial discussion that in my experience, the bigger challenge is not in how to use the retirement plan as an investing vehicle, but how to find the right property. That property is one that will generate great double-digit yields and require little effort to manage or remodel before it begins to produce a profit for the retirement plan. The "finding the right property" challenge will always be present, while simply taking title to the property in the IRA will become second nature. Avoiding prohibited transactions will also become second nature once you spend a little time understanding the rules.

What are these prohibited transactions?

Internal Revenue Code 4975(c)(1) and IRS Publication 590 explain that every transaction the IRA engages in, must be for the exclusive benefit of the retirement plan. A CPA or tax attorney will often refer to these transactions as "self-dealing" transactions. This section of the Code identifies prohibited transactions to include any direct or indirect:

- Selling, exchanging or leasing of any asset or property between your retirement plan and a disqualified person. For example, you cannot use your IRA to buy property you currently own from you.

- Dealing with income or assets of a plan by a disqualified person who is a fiduciary acting in his own interest or for his own account. For example, you cannot under the rules, loan money to your CPA or attorney.

- Lending money or providing credit to your retirement plan or a plan owned by a disqualified person. For example, your IRA cannot loan money to your spouse who is clearly a disqualified party.

- Furnishing goods, services or facilities between your plan and a disqualified person. For example, you cannot rent a property owned by your IRA to your children or to your parents.

- Using or receiving benefit from an asset owned by your retirement plan. For example, your IRA cannot buy a vacation home you or a disqualified party intends to use.

- Receiving any consideration for your personal account in connection with a transaction involving the income or assets of the plan. For example, you cannot pay yourself a management fee from income generated from a rental property owned by your retirement plan.

One of the primary advantages of using self-directed custodians or administrators is that they are very familiar with the IRS rules governing retirement plans. Before you get too far into a transaction, it's always a good idea to review your intended investment with your custodian. Their websites typically provide an overview of the rules so you can better understand the type of transactions that are both permissible and prohibited.

Although it's always a good idea to seek guidance from personal tax advisors, know that unless they have experience with self-directed retirement plans, their initial advice may be that the rules are too complicated or that they don't want to provide advice in an area in which they have little experience.

In chapter 14 we describe the benefits of building a solid team of advisers. Having a tax professional who is experienced in self-directed retirement plans will help you avoid prohibited transactions.

Chapter 16.3

WHO ARE THESE DISQUALIFIED PARTIES?

The IRS rules identifying the businesses with which your IRA can transact business may leave you wondering what Congress was smoking the day they started setting guidelines in this area. If you go back to the intent they may have had, however, it becomes more understandable. At the end of the day, these retirement plans were designed to provide a savings plan that would keep account holders off government-provided assistance programs; so making the restrictions on doing business with certain family members a good idea.

For example, the rules prohibit your IRA from doing business with any linear relative; this includes your parents and grandparents as well as your children or grandchildren. Every summer, I receive calls from IRA owners who explain that a son or daughter is headed off to another year at college and wants to live off campus with a few roommates. Thus, Mom and Dad have decided to make a real estate investment in a rental property near campus, using their IRA funds.

Most of these investors have read the rules and feel there must be a way to accomplish their new goal while not breaking the rules. Although there *might be* some "creative" way to put together a "transaction" that may *look* legitimate, at the end of the day you are violating the IRS rules if any benefit whatsoever, other than a financial benefit, is received by the account owner. Some may argue, "This is purely a financial benefit" since I was about to pay for student housing (an expense) and now, as the account owner, I'll instead be receiving income off the students who pay us rent. The problem is that one of the renters is a linear relative. A family member is benefiting from your retirement account and this would clearly be a prohibited transaction.

My guess is that Congress felt most account owners would sacrifice the funds in their account before evicting a family member living in a property owned by the retirement plan, if the rents couldn't be paid. Or, Congress saw a loophole some would exploit by buying a home with IRA funds, letting their retired parents move in and never collecting rental income. In this case, regardless of who occupies the home, the account owner has, *in effect*, taken a withdrawal from the account and avoided the taxes and possible penalties that would be due upon distribution.

The perplexing part of the rules that relate to doing business with family members is that brothers and sisters are not considered linear relatives. Because of this, I'm sure there are IRA owners who often do business with their siblings and repeatedly enjoy profitable transactions.

For the complete definition of who is considered a "disqualified party," please reference Internal Revenue Code (IRC) 4975(e) (1).

The list includes:

- The IRA owner
- The IRA owner's spouse
- Ancestors (Mom, Dad, grandparents)
- Linear descendents (daughters, sons, grandchildren)
- Spouses of linear descendants (son or daughter-in-law)

Non-Family Members who are disqualified parties

Yes, there are others who cannot engage in business transactions with your retirement account, including:

- Investment advisors
- Fiduciaries – those providing services to the plan
- Any business entity i.e., LLC, corporation, trust or partnership in which any of the disqualified persons mentioned above has an ownership interest.

So if, for example, your CPA offers you a great buy on a rental property he owns, be sure to check with your custodian before you agree to purchase the property in your IRA. You should not allow your IRA to do business with anyone providing financial advice.

Step Transactions

If you are one of those people who love finding a ways around the rules, regardless of who wrote them or what the penalties look like, you might be thinking, "Aha! I'll rent that college townhome to my sister, who will in turn rent it to my son when he's off at school." Nice try. What you've just described is commonly called a "Step Transaction".

Any good CPA or tax attorney will tell you that whenever you create a series of separate but related transactions, they may be viewed as a single transaction designed to circumvent the IRS rules. Be very careful whenever you get creative in your IRA transactions. The penalties for violating these rules can be severe. Always check with your tax adviser as well as your IRA custodian before entering into a transaction that may be considered a prohibited transaction. There are so many good opportunities available that are nowhere close to being considered a "gray area" that it really isn't necessary for you to take the risk of violating the rules.

Conclusion

It's surprising to me how many investors will completely give up on the idea of owning real estate in their retirement plan if their first attempt takes them into an area considered a prohibited transaction. They get frustrated that the rules prohibit them from buying property from their parents or from renting to their children. Instead of investing their energy into looking at other opportunities they spend it cursing the IRS, and their savings dwindle away in bank CDs or mutual funds. The easy path to investing your retirement savings into Wall Street investments may often be the least profitable path to take.

Chapter 16.4

I'VE BROKEN THE RULES-NOW WHAT?

If you find yourself in a position where a prohibited transaction has occurred in your retirement account you need to take immediate action. Taking the position that the IRS may never discover the mistake is a recipe for disaster at some later date. Stepping forward to notify the IRS of the violation should be discussed with your Custodian and tax advisor.

In most cases you'll be advised to reverse the transaction as soon as possible and disclose the rule violation by filing an amended tax return which will report any taxable income that may have occurred as a result of the prohibited transaction. Be sure to seek advice from an experienced tax advisor who has worked with clients on similar situations.

At the end of the day the IRS is interested in collecting the taxes and possible penalties for an early withdrawal from the retirement plan. Although every prohibited transaction case is slightly different and the IRS can be unpredictable, stories of IRA account seizure are rare and often exaggerations of what typically occurs if you step forward and take action to correct any mistake that occurred.

Chapter 16.5

VALUATION OF ASSETS IN THE IRA

The custodian of your self-directed IRA will require a fair market valuation each year on all assets held in the account. This fair market valuation is used to establish the year-end value of each asset in the account and provides for proper tax reporting to the IRS. If you have an IRA with a bank or brokerage firm they can easily calculate the value of the assets based upon the closing prices of each security on the last trading day of the year.

When it comes to establishing a year-end value for non-publicly traded assets, the custodian will request that you as the account owner provide the value of the asset. Custodian set their own requirements on whether the valuation comes from the account owner or if a third-party opinion is necessary. Typically, the asset valuations become more important when the account owner reaches age 70 ½ since this is when the Required Minimum Distributions (RMDs) begin. See Chapter 3 for more on RMDs.

Real Estate

Real estate valuations can be provided in a few different ways. The most inexpensive approach is to use a licensed real estate broker who is at arm's length to you and your investment property. The broker can provide you with an "opinion of value" letter based upon comparable sales. Typically, these opinions are free of charge.

Formal appraisals are also acceptable; however, the preparation of these reports on an annual basis may prove to be expensive in relation to the value of the property. Often the custodian will be satisfied with a valuation letter signed by the account owner which describes the method used in arriving at the annual reported property value.

Private Stock –Limited Liability Company shares

Each asset owned by the Corporation or limited liability company (LLC) must be valued and the debt, if any, must be subtracted to arrive at a per-share net asset value. Real estate can be evaluated using the methods noted in the above section. Other assets can be valued using information reported on the company's annual tax return. Custodians are commonly satisfied when the company's chief financial officer provides a value on the shares titled in the name of the retirement plan.

Private Placements

The manager of your private placement investment will provide the value for your investment at the end of each tax year. Most importantly, it is your responsibility to obtain this information and provide it to your custodian on the required reporting forms.

Precious Metals and Brokerage Accounts

Valuations for these assets are found on the annual statements provided by the brokerage firm or third-party depository that is holding the precious metals.

Mortgages and Promissory Notes

Custodians are typically comfortable using the face value of any notes or mortgages held in the IRA as adequate records for account value reporting.

Of course, any uninvested cash that is in your IRA at year-end is added to the value of all other assets to arrive at the final account balance for IRS reporting requirements.

Most custodians will send account owners a reminder notice in November to report their asset values within a few weeks of the year-end period. All good custodians make the reporting process as easy as possible.

It's a good idea to inquire about the custodian's annual reporting requirements during the interview process before you select a custodian for your self-directed account. Request a copy of the form you'll be expected to complete and deliver to the custodian each year. All the custodians I recommend are focused on providing a high level of customer service with minimal effort on the part of the client. (see chapter 4.1 for tips on selecting a custodian)

Chapter 17

INVESTING WITH OTHER PEOPLES IRA ACCOUNTS

If you are like most investors who discover the Self Directed IRA method of investing you'll share your experiences with those you care about. Nearly everyone I know who has tasted the sweet success of making tax-free profits from an investment they selected can't keep this a secret very long and they tell everyone who will listen to their story, especially those investors who complain about their lack of investing success and truly need to make a change.

Often these stories lead to a discussion about how the uninitiated investor can join you in the next opportunity you discover. It's only natural that others, who know you well, will be interested in joining in on the success you've created.

Investing with friends and family members can be difficult if they are going to hold you responsible for the outcome of every risk they take. However, most people with any investing experience realize that at the end of the day they have to take risks before they can realize a return and that just because you've had success in the past it doesn't guarantee they will as well.

You'll need to decide if you are more comfortable sharing the next investment opportunity that comes along or if you want to limit you role to simply educating others on the advantages of the Self Directed retirement plan and letting them pursue their own investing ideas.

Most of us eventually reach a limit on the number of investments we can hold in our retirement plans based upon available capital in the account. That's when you'll need to decide whether to begin bringing in partners in order to expand the profits you are earning or diversify the holdings in your account. Personally I'd rather own 20% of five properties vs.

100% of just one. Everyone has a different view on diversification and how much control they want to individually maintain when it comes to their investment holdings.

If you've discovered an opportunity that is beyond your individual financial capability, you may want to consider sharing the risks as well as the rewards by partnering with other investors. When your circle of family and friends isn't large enough to fully finance your next venture, you may have no other option but to attract outside investors. With banks becoming more stringent on their lending criteria for real estate investors as well as start-up companies, many entrepreneurs are obtaining all or a portion of their financing from Self-Directed retirement plans.

Below are just a few of the most common ways you can attract financing from those who want to invest their retirement plans typically into local ventures with people they trust.

- **Partner:** Your IRA funds are combined with another investor's funds to buy an asset
- **Borrow:** You or your IRA borrows funds from an investor or their IRA account
- **Borrow with a profit share agreement:** You or your IRA pays interest plus a percentage of the profits to an investor or their IRA
- **Sell shares in your Corporation or LLC:** IRA investor accounts purchase a percentage of your business
- **Buy-Fix-Sell or Rent:** IRA investor accounts invest in real estate with you as the manager, so the investor isn't required to find, repair or manage tenants

Chapter 17.3 describes how to successfully work with investors who don't know you but desire to invest with you. Always seek competent legal advice from a securities attorney before agreeing to accept investment capital from an investor regardless of your relationship with the investor.

Chapter 17.1

STEPS TO BECOMING A SUCCESSFUL BORROWER FROM IRA INVESTORS

So you have a great investment opportunity and all you need is a little extra capital to get started? Whether you are working on a real estate transaction or funding a business, you'll discover that retirement plan investors can be an excellent source of capital. So often these investors have learned that by managing their own funds into deals where they have some hands-on past experience, they make not only higher returns but also face less risk vs. investing on the advice of a broker into Wall Street products.

Generally, these investors are experienced enough to know that what's most important *is not the return on the investment but the return of their investment that matters the most.* Because of this, you'll be adding more than just capital to your venture; you'll be bringing in a silent partner who will often work with you in ways to promote and foster the success of your project.

Open yourself up to the idea that some of these investors may have valuable suggestions on how to structure the deal into a win/win long-term relationship. Imagine having a small group of investors you can turn to for funding, a group that can also act as an unofficial Board of Directors willing to offer expertise and contacts in order for your venture to grow, as well as to protect their investment funds.

This is often the nature of the relationship that develops between entrepreneur and retirement plan investor over time. In my experience, these self-directed investors are always looking for good opportunities with self-motivated entrepreneurs. They need you as much as you need them, and they are looking for you and the opportunity you have created right now, more than ever.

Before we jump into presenting your opportunity and getting the funding you are seeking, we need to face a few facts. The vast majority of investors with retirement accounts have never heard of taking control of their IRA or 401(k) and using the self- directed method of investing. Unfortunately, it is estimated that only two percent of the retirement plans in existence today are self-directed. The number of these accounts is growing at a rate of several hundred new accounts per day however; many of the investors you'll speak with will need a basic education on how they can join the ranks of the self-directed movement. You could always give them this book to help launch their education, as well as introduce them to the custodians you have chosen to use.

All of the major self-directed custodian companies provide a great deal of educational help on their websites. Some investors new to this concept will do a tremendous amount of research into the IRS rules, the various account options and the custodian fees, while others will be quick to see the benefits and want to begin taking control of their options.

Often it just comes down to how much pain they have experienced with the poor performance of Wall Street investing methods and whether they realize how little time they have to build a retirement plan they can count on in the future. Regardless of how motivated investors are to make changes to the performance of their retirement plan, they will be looking to you for basic educational information on how these self-directed accounts work.

You need to be prepared to answer the common questions on self-directed IRAs and recommend a custodian for their account. If you haven't opened a self-directed account yourself and you are suggesting a friend invest with you through their retirement plan, be prepared to be asked this question: "If this is so good why haven't you gone with a self-directed retirement account?"

It's a fair question, so I always advise those seeking capital to have their own account established, even if it's a small account. By going through the new account opening process yourself and making a contribution to the account or transferring your old IRA account into the new account, you will gain some valuable first hand experience you can share with others who may invest with you or loan you funds from their IRA.

Although it would be ideal to recommend the same custodian to every potential lender/ investor you encounter, having a few custodian relationships is a good idea in case the primary custodian you suggest doesn't make the investor comfortable. Investors have been known to reject a custodian on less than rational reasons. Maybe your investor's ex-mother-in-law is from the city the custodian is located in, so the investor rejects the entire self-directed concept (and your opportunity) based upon some unrelated past experience.

Become familiar with several custodians as well as their new account forms before you begin to look for funding. Most of the time, your investor (if new to the self- directed concept) is going to take your recommendation on which custodian to use, especially if it's the firm you are using for your own account. This becomes even more important if your IRA is seeking a loan from your investor's IRA. The transaction between IRA accounts is faster and easier if a single custodian is overseeing the documents and transfer of funds between two clients of their firm.

Again, your goal is to create a true win/win relationship with your investors. This begins with making it easy for them to become educated, open their self-directed account and begin earning an attractive return.

Chapter 17.2

HOW TO BORROW FROM IRAS TO FUND YOUR REAL ESTATE OR GROWING BUSINESS

For well over 25 years now, IRA account owners have been making loans to real estate investors and entrepreneurs in need of capital to fund their growing businesses. Most investors doing this today have learned easy methods to make loans from their retirement plans in order to receive higher returns when working with an experienced real estate investor or entrepreneur.

These lender/borrower relationships are a win/win solution for both parties. The investor typically receives an interest rate several times higher than they would earn in a money market account or CD, and the borrower can get quick access to loans without the long and expensive lending process required at banks.

Benefits to the Borrower

Why would you want to borrow from an investor's IRA vs. a traditional bank?

- You can meet and negotiate directly with the lender vs. the bank's loan committee.
- You get to structure the loan to your needs vs. fitting into a pre-defined bank program.
- The property secures the loan vs. your credit score, personal guarantee or current income levels.
- IRA lenders don't place a cap on your ability to borrow for future deals vs. the tendency of a bank to do so.
- IRS lenders may not charge fees vs. banks who have a practice

of charging fees for credit checks, document fees, appraisal fees, etc.

- Your payment schedule to the lender can be structured to fit your individual needs vs. the bank dictating when payments are due.

Benefits to the Lender

- Higher returns vs. the stock, bond, mutual fund market
- Higher returns than the historically low yields on money market funds and CDs currently paid by banks.
- Safety in knowing where the retirement funds are invested. The security on a loan can be the first mortgage on a property or other assets well understood by the lender.
- The IRA account owner is doing business with someone the lender has met and trusts.
- It is easier to monitor the value of the collateral that secures an IRA's loan
- Diversification away from Wall Street investments and over to Main Street type investments in the lender's own community.

How do borrowers and lenders find each other?

It's not as hard as you may initially think to find either a borrower or an IRA lender. Over the last several years, IRA custodians have been hosting more events that attract both borrowers and lenders. This is often where parties meet to begin a transaction.

IRA custodians have to be extra careful to avoid any type of matchmaking service since they are prohibited from making investment recommendations. However, while providing a valuable educational service to their retirement plan clients through these events, they are also providing a forum where, with a little networking effort, you'll meet many of the types of people you are searching for.

I suggest getting on the mailing list for all of the larger IRA custodian companies. They offer either an annual educational event or a series of informal local events designed to teach clients how to manage their self-directed retirement plans and find good investment opportunities.

If you are a lender looking for a borrower, consider:

- Advertising in your local newspaper - be specific on the kind of loans you'll make
- Speaking with CPAs, mortgage brokers, financial planners - let them know what you can offer their clients.
- Talking with Realtors – they often know of real estate investors seeking funding for a local property
- Local private lenders who can often refer borrowers to you when they are unable to make a loan themselves
- Networking with other IRA lenders across the country
- Looking at internet-based matchmakers that connect lenders to borrowers

If you are a borrower looking for a lender, in addition to the above list, consider;

- Making a list of everyone you know who may have a retirement plan; share what you have learned about self-directed IRAs
- Joining your local Real Estate Investor Club
- Offering to present your opportunities at custodian educational events

With a little networking, you'll discover there are more opportunities out there than you have time to research. If you are an investor, look into businesses you understand and have experience with. If you are a borrower, seek out people who have a connection with your industry who can understand the opportunity you have created.

Chapter 17.3

BUILDING YOUR CREDIBILITY KIT

It's only natural that most entrepreneurs seeking a loan or investment capital from retirement plan investors are going to begin their search by contacting friends or colleagues with your opportunity. Often, depending on how much capital you need to get your venture launched, you'll never need to attract funding from people who are complete strangers. Eventually, however, you will find yourself speaking or meeting with an investor or lender who knows nothing about you, and you'll need to sell them on not only your *project* but on who you are. I have found that doing some advanced preparation pays big dividends and that having a Credibility Kit" makes all the difference in the world.

The Credibility Kit is a printed presentation that tells the story about you, your goals and your past successes in life, as well as the project you wish to finance. The kit is often assembled in a 3-ring binder because, as you'll see in a moment, you'll likely be adding information to the kit over time so having the ability to add pages will be important. It's often a good idea to use tabs to separate each section of the kit so that it's easy for the investor to review specific sections.

The details on the property you wish to finance or the company you want to fund are placed in the latter half of the kit. Investors want to know about "you" as much or more than they want to understand the deal you are offering. You'll have to decide how much you want to share about yourself, however, the more information you provide the better the results.

The credibility kit is best used in a face-to-face meeting with your potential investor. You won't go through every page and into tremendous details, but you'll want to make it clear that if the investor is interested in your proposal, you'll be leaving the kit with them to review.

You Credibility Kit should contain;

- Your current resume or information on the work you've done, even if it's not related to real estate or your current venture
- Copies of all awards and diplomas
- Newspaper articles about you - anything that tells about your life
- Information on past properties - purchase and sale-closing statements
- Picture of current and past properties showing you and other lenders/investors
- Copy of your life insurance policy
- Insurance polices on your investment properties
- Information on your charitable work or community service
- Pictures of your home and family
- Copy of your current financial statement
- Copy of your recent tax return
- Letters of recommendation
- Your long-term goal list or "bucket" list
- Your hobbies

Project information:

- Sample copy of the mortgage or loan agreement
- Copy of the purchase agreement, if you already own the property
- Appraisal report and comparable property values
- Location map of the property
- Lease agreement your tenants will sign, if you are funding a rental property
- Sample property management agreement, if you intend to use a manager
- Income statement or financial projection for the property or venture
- Pictures of the property that will secure the investor loan
- Business plan if you are funding a business venture
- Articles on the market area of the property or your industry

Yes, it can take some time to compile all of the above information; however, you'll find that investors will be impressed by your focus on the details and your willingness to disclose as much as you have about your background. The Credibility Kit helps to build a bond with your investor, and you'll likely find that you have many things in common, as you share your story with them.

Chapter 17.4

BUILDING CREDIBILITY WITH YOUR INVESTORS

Here is a quick story about a client who achieved success using the Credibility Kit:

Nancy is a nurse, caring for people her entire life. She *enjoys* nursing, even with the long hours, and although she earns a good living, she sees the benefits of building a large retirement plan for the future. She began her real estate investing career a few years ago and has always put her focus on providing housing to tenants that were older and in need of a home close to the hospital where she works. She knows the needs of elderly tenants so when she buys property she will often make minor modifications in order to provide her tenants with easier entry and exit to the home. She'll often remodel the bathrooms and kitchens so that they are more user- friendly for her elderly tenants. Her rental property business is an extension of her experience in the healthcare industry. This is the market she knows best, and that's one of the reasons she has been so successful.

Nancy also uses the Credibility Kit to introduce herself to new lenders. Whenever she finds a new property to add to her portfolio, she updates the kit with all the property details as soon as her offer is accepted by the property seller. She then begins making calls to investors with whom she has discussed her business while networking with her friends at the hospital.

If you were to leaf through Nancy's Credibility Kit, you'd see she is married to Hank who teaches at the local high school and coaches the men's track team. She has three daughters. Her youngest is a junior in high school while the two older girls are in college. The family often spends their summer vacation time at the beach. Nancy's biggest goals are to continue providing a good education to her girls and retire with plenty of savings.

Information on her current and past rental properties is included in her Credibility Kit, along with "before and after" pictures showing the improvements to the homes. Because she understands how valuable a testimonial letter can be to a new lender, Nancy has requested and received a letter of recommendation from all of her past real estate lenders. The copies of the life insurance policies included in her Credibility Kit provide evidence to each lender that if anything were to happen to Nancy, the policy would be sufficient to pay off the mortgages on the rental properties.

Before she meets with a new potential lender, she'll have prepared a budget of the remodeling costs of the new property and will include the written estimates for the contractor she plans to hire. She also includes a copy of her recent IRA statement, which helps justify her recommendation that her new investor use the same custodian that she has used for many years.

Nearly every possible question an investor would ever think to ask is answered in her Credibility Kit.

Sure, you can find lenders who will work with you and fund your projects without ever seeing a Credibility Kit. The majority of the real estate investors I've met find a way to get their financing from contacts they've made. However, they spend a great deal of time looking for investors, and they miss out on good deals because of their limited access to capital. The time they spend on chasing after funding would be better spent on shopping for more profitable opportunities to own in their retirement plan.

Eventually you can build a list of investors who are excited to be a part of your next opportunity, and you'll rely less and less on the Credibility Kit.

If you'd like to learn more about creating your Credibility Kit visit: www.IRAassets.com and place **Credibility Kit** in the search box. I will send you a free report on how this tool can help you accelerate your project funding.

Chapter 18

WHAT COMES FIRST? SHOULD I LOOK FOR THE MONEY OR THE DEAL?

So often, IRA investors who feel they will need a partner or a lender will ask me about whether they should initially focus their efforts on finding an investor or finding a good investment property. The answer depends on a couple of factors. If you are well connected and have a good list of potential lenders or partners, I'd suggest you look for a good property with above-average profit potential. At the same time, if great deals are everywhere you look and you are just beginning to build your network of investors, it's time to start putting your energy into finding investors. In other words, work on the area where you are experiencing a shortage.

Granted, it can be difficult to explain to investors that you don't have specific property to discuss with them and that all you want to share is the general concept of using retirement plan funds to invest in real estate or a business opportunity you are researching; however, keep in mind that if your investor is new to the self-directed concept, you can typically expect 30 to 60 days to go by before that investor will have opened a self-directed account and completed the transfer of funds from the old retirement plan custodian into the new, self-directed account.

In many cases, the investor who has never heard of self-directed investing is going to be reluctant to move funds to a new account until seen in the details of what you can offer in terms of annual yields, as well as the safety of the investment. If you find yourself in this position, your initial goal should be to at least have your investor open the account even if you have to pay the $100 new account fee. At least the new account will be opened and the transfer of funds from the current custodian to the new custodian shouldn't take more than two-three weeks.

If you already have a good list of potential investors who believe in you, then of course it's time to find a few good deals. I say a few, because if you have experience in real estate you know often you can be out-bid on a property or for whatever reason the seller just takes someone else's offer over yours. Some experts that teach advanced real estate investing will recommend making close to 100 offers to land one deal. Now that sounds excessive, however, if you are out there making offers at 60% of the asking price, it may take that many offers to get an accepted contract. That all depends on your market and the type of property you are seeking.

Too often I speak with the New Real Estate investor who is focused on buying bank-owned properties or short-sale opportunities. They often give up after the bank turns down the initial offer or the bank's response takes weeks to come in. Yes, it's disappointing when your offer is rejected; however, you need to <u>expect to fail more than you succeed when you make below market rate offers that will generate a high yield or large eventual gains</u>.

The most successful real estate investors I know are always on the lookout for both good deals as well as capital. Having several investors waiting in the wings while you shop for property is a good problem to have. Some are going to be willing to wait while others will find another home for their capital.

The biggest mistake I see new IRA investors make, if they need partners or lenders to build their portfolio, is to not begin building an investor list until they find the perfect property. They feel they don't have anything to present, so why go to the effort of meeting lenders or investors? Well, you have to sell yourself and your abilities, long before you sell someone on the opportunity you've discovered. Successful investor meetings can begin by explaining, "I don't have an investment to talk with you about today. I want to share my business model with you and if you like it, I'll be in touch when I have something that may fit your needs." This takes the pressure off of everyone and leads to the development of much better relationships.

A few times a year I teach a class with one of the large IRA custodian firms called "How to Fund your Real Estate Deals or Growing Business with IRA Investors." If you'd like to learn more, just register at: www.IRAassets (if you haven't already) and enter "Find IRA Investors" in the **More Info** box. You'll receive a free report on the courses offered on this topic.

Chapter 19

OWNING A BUSINESS IN YOUR RETIREMENT PLAN

The concept of owning a business that is funded by your IRA or 401k plan has to be the most controversial topic in the self-directed retirement plan industry today. With corporate downsizing forcing many experienced business managers into the ranks of the unemployed, these people often want to test their entrepreneurial skills by funding their own start-up company or simply buying an existing business using their retirement plan.

This chapter is just an overview on this concept and is not intended to provide a full examination on the risks or rewards of owning a business in your retirement plan.

You can separate the self-directed retirement plan industry experts into three groups, all based upon their opinions as to whether the IRS will allow these kinds of investments.

There are those who believe that owning a business that pays you or any family member a salary or any type of compensation for your efforts in managing the business is a clear violation of the IRS rules.

Another group sees this type of an investment as a grey area within the rules and will tell you that, to date, there just aren't enough IRS court decisions to make a clear judgment on what you can or cannot do when it comes to owning a business inside your retirement plan.

Then there is the group of experts who make a strong argument in favor of this type of retirement plan investment as long as you follow their recipe for success. As you might imagine, those who are proponents of this activity are also the people who market a system that will, in their opinion, allow you to work within the IRS guidelines and avoid going to war with the IRS.

Without question, if you are considering using any type of retirement plan that has been funded to provide you future benefits or to fund a business that may benefit you in any way, you should seek the advice of your personal CPA or tax attorney. Don't be surprised to receive conflicting advice in this area, since again there have not been many court cases to clearly define what you can and cannot do when it comes to owning a business that is funded by your retirement plan and also pays you a salary or any type of compensation for your efforts.

The key question to ask your self is, "Do I expect to receive any benefit over and above what any other investor in the company will receive?" If the answer is "No, my retirement plan is strictly a shareholder or lender to the company, and I will have no involvement in the operation of the company," then I believe you are making an ordinary retirement plan investment that is not different from owning shares of any publicly-traded company.

However, if you see yourself receiving any form of benefit from the work you do or the advice you share with the management team of the company, I believe you have moved into that grey area of the IRS rules. Why would the IRS have an issue with you receiving compensation in exchange for your labor, management or advice? Of course the income you are paid would be reported as earnings, and you'd be taxed on that income just like any other compensation. Right?

Well the IRS knows there are some very creative people who do everything they can to find every loophole in the rules. The IRS may have various issues with you funding your business with retirement plan savings however I feel their main concern is this:

The funds in most retirement plans have not been taxed as earnings when they were deposited into the plan, or the retirement plan owner has received a deduction from their taxable earnings when the funds were deposited by the taxpayer. The IRS expects to collect the tax when the account owner receives a distribution from the retirement account, and it expects to collect an additional penalty tax if the account owner receives the income before the age of 59 ½ years of age. So you can see that someone wanting to avoid the early withdrawal penalty could simply place his retirement plan into a company that then pays a salary, or any other type of compensation, as a way to dodge the penalty.

Many clients over the years have considered buying a business for their children or other family members and financing it from the retirement plan. Keep in mind there are prohibited transaction rules you must adhere to when a family member may stand to benefit in any way from the account holders retirement plan. See Chapter 16.2 on prohibited transaction rules.

For example, Greg has enjoyed a successful career as a salesperson for a large chemical company in Maine. His employer provided a 401k plan, and Greg always took advantage of it by fully funding it each year. The company's stock, which Greg continued to buy in the plan, preformed very well over the years. Greg's son Terry, who gained experience working on fishing boats while in high school, told his dad he wanted to buy a boat and go into business for himself, so Greg wanted to help by financing the boat purchase.

Unfortunately, the prohibited transaction rules kept Greg from using his retirement plan as an investor since his son would be benefiting as a result of the transaction. As we covered in the prohibited transaction rule section, your retirement plan cannot do business with family members. Greg's plan to finance his son's fishing business would be very much like buying a rental property and letting his son pay rent to occupy the home. Even if a fair market rent was paid by the family member, the rules prohibit this type of investment.

With all of this said, if you are determined to own and manage a business and fund it with your retirement plan, you should do further research and speak to the companies who specialize in helping clients accomplish this goal. They will explain that instead of seeking traditional small business financing or franchise financing, many entrepreneurs and business owners have funded their business by rolling their existing retirement funds into a new corporation without tax penalties. The new corporation then buys the business or pays the franchise fees and begins operations. As profits are earned in the business, they are paid into the retirement plan without being taxed, just like dividends are not taxed when paid each year into an IRA or 401k plan account.

In summary, it is very clear that your retirement plan can invest into a start-up or well established business of any size, as long as you the account owner have the potential of receiving a financial benefit only and nothing more. Expect to see more IRS rulings in the area of investing your retirement plan into a business that also offers you employment or benefits over and above those that a passive investor would be expected to receive. Of course you should seek competent tax advice before you invest your retirement funds in this area. Carefully research any new IRS rulings in this area before making a final decision.

Chapter 20

TIME TO GET STARTED

If you've turned to the back of the book to see how the story ends.... well, this is really the beginning of your own story, and it's easy to create a success story for yourself, your retirement plan and those you care about the most. The most common reaction from investors who just bought real estate or any other alternative asset in their retirement plans is, "Wow! That was easy! Why didn't I do this years ago??" They say the exact same thing when they sell an asset owned by the retirement plan, with even more enthusiasm because they are not paying taxes immediately on the gains made from the sale.

As I covered earlier, the primary reason to manage your own retirement plan is that you are in far more control over the assets you place in the plan. Getting that control can come at a cost. You have to make a commitment to yourself that you'll invest the time to manage the assets in your plan. It's a small price to pay when compared to just blindly trusting your future and your retirement plans to someone who cares far less about the outcome or performance of your investment portfolio than you do.

"Invest in what you know" is the motto for many smart investors. It's good advice from what I've seen. You can do this regardless of how busy you think you might be. With today's technologies, it is far easier to manage a portfolio of properties than it was just five years ago. Take it one step at a time and surround yourself with an experienced team to help you on your first few transactions. When you've gotten good at this, I encourage you to share the ideas you've learned with those you care about.

Thanks for making an investment in yourself, and I trust you've benefited from what was shared in this book. There is no better time than the present to take inventory of your retirement goals and develop a clear success plan you can follow. If you haven't opened a self-directed IRA yet, that's the first step in writing your own success story.

Good Luck and share your success story with us.

Visit: www.IRAassets.com for all the news on self directing your retirement plans.

Additional Resources

Peter Fortunato of St.Petersburg, Florida, (www.peterfortunato.com)

Dykes Boddiford - Guerrilla Bankruptcy Tactics for Creditors (1998) (http://assets101.com/)

Jackie Lange – Creative Real Estate Investing (http://www.cashflowdepot.com)

Sidney L. Chase Sr.- *No Bull Real Estate* (2009) (http://sydchase.com)

John T.Reed - *How to Buy Real Estate for At Least 20% Below Market Value(2007) How to Manage Residential Property for Maximum Cash Flow and Resale Value (1998)*

David Tilney –Hassle Free Property Management (http://davidtilney.com)

INDEX

1031 exchange rules	136
Administrators	30, 88-89, 98, 101, 165, 170
Agricultural Land	54, 128-129
Agriculture	78, 114, 128
Albert Einstein	48
Alternative Energy	114, 121
American Association of Retired Persons (AARP)	33
Baby Boomers	23-24, 31-34
Benjamin Franklin	43, 105
Bernie Madoff	91
Boettner Center for Retirement Research	23
Boomers	23-24, 31-34
Checkbook IRA	57, 93-94, 105-109
Collectibles	30, 79, 81-82
Commercial Properties	127
Congress	26, 52-54, 70, 164, 171-172
Corporation	30, 72-73, 79, 83, 97, 172, 179, 196
Credibility Kit	186-190
Dale Carnegie	55
David Tilney	201
Death Benefit	69
Deeds of Trust	77-79
Dennis Miller	52
Development Land	128
Dykes Boddiford	201
Equity Trust Company	90
Eviction Procedures	162
Federal Deposit Insurance Corporation (FDIC)	83
First-Time Homebuyer Benefit	68
Hawaiian Punch	143
Henry Ford	29
Horizon Trust Company	90

Individual-K	73
In-Service Rollover	57, 100-103
International Real Estate	129-130
IRA Club	90
IRAassets.com	19, 30, 94, 190, 199
IRS.gov	46, 75
Jackie Lange	201
Jerry Seinfeld	164
Jim Rohn	41
John Maynard Keynes	50
John T. Reed	126, 201
Lease Options	131
Life Insurance	30, 79, 81, 187, 190
Limited Liability Company (LLC)	105, 107, 176
Limited Partnerships	78
Marina-boat Slips	131
Michael Jordan	155
Mortgages	30, 46, 78-79, 83, 114, 120, 176, 190
Movie *Inside Job*	27
Multi-family Homes	127
New Direction IRA, Inc.	89
Non-Collectible Hard Assets	114
Oil and Gas	78, 102, 114, 120-121
Partnerships	56, 78, 81, 114, 123-124
Peter Fortunato	131, 201
Peter G. Peterson	26
Precious Metals	18, 46, 51, 53, 68, 78, 82-85, 91, 93, 103, 114, 118, 120, 176
Private Business Ownership	114
Private Equity	114
Private Notes	78
Prohibited Transactions	124, 143-144, 168-170
Promissory Notes	114, 120, 176
Property Manager	45, 58, 95, 139-142, 147, 154, 156, 158-163

QuickBooks	107
Ralph Waldo Emerson	26
Real estate agent-Broker	56, 76, 95, 130, 141, 153, 156, 159-161
RMD (Required Minimum Distribution)	148
Roth Individual-(k)	74
Roth IRA	54, 66-74, 137, 145, 148
Running on Empty	27
SEP IRA	66-68, 70-72, 85
Short-Sale Opportunities	192
Sidney L. Chase Sr.	201
Simple IRA	29, 66-73
Social Security	24, 31-32, 85
Solo 401(k)	67, 73-74, 93
Standard & Poor's 500	23
Summit Trust Company	90
Tax liens	78-79, 83, 109
Tenants	45, 126-128, 158-159, 162-163, 179, 187, 189
The Seven Habits of Highly Successful People	150
Title-Escrow Agent	156
Tony Robbins	116
United Airlines Bankruptcy	97
Vacation Homes	130, 141
Venture Capital	78, 114, 118, 121-123
Warren Buffett	35, 38
William Shakespeare	59
www.VRBO.com	140